Anthony Savio Herminio da Piedade Fernandes

WISDOM IN THE WORD

Anthony Savio Herminio da Piedade Fernandes

WISDOM IN THE WORD

Life Lessons from Biblical Stories

Blessed Hope Publishing

Imprint

Any brand names and product names mentioned in this book are subject to trademark, brand or patent protection and are trademarks or registered trademarks of their respective holders. The use of brand names, product names, common names, trade names, product descriptions etc. even without a particular marking in this work is in no way to be construed to mean that such names may be regarded as unrestricted in respect of trademark and brand protection legislation and could thus be used by anyone.

Cover image: www.ingimage.com

Publisher:
Blessed Hope Publishing
is a trademark of
Dodo Books Indian Ocean Ltd. and OmniScriptum S.R.L publishing group

120 High Road, East Finchley, London, N2 9ED, United Kingdom
Str. Armeneasca 28/1, office 1, Chisinau MD-2012, Republic of Moldova, Europe
Printed at: see last page
ISBN: 978-620-4-18833-1

WISDOM IN THE WORD

LIFE LESSONS FROM BIBLICAL STORIES

By

Anthony Savio Herminio da Piedade Fernandes

[MFS, M.Com (F&C), M.Com (Accountancy), MA (PS), SET, NET]

PREFACE

In the labyrinth of life, where decisions often seem overwhelming and the path forward can appear uncertain, many seek guidance from various sources to navigate their way. Among the myriad resources available, the Bible stands out as a profound wellspring of wisdom, offering solace, direction, and insight. This book, "Wisdom in the Word: Life Lessons from Biblical Stories," aims to illustrate how the timeless teachings of the Bible can address contemporary challenges and provide clarity in moments of confusion.

The premise of this collection is rooted in the belief that the Bible, with its rich tapestry of stories and teachings, remains a relevant and powerful tool for personal growth and decision-making. Each story in this book is crafted to reflect how biblical principles can be applied to everyday situations, showing that the wisdom of ancient scriptures can guide us through modern dilemmas.

The Relevance of Biblical Wisdom

In an age where information is abundant yet wisdom seems scarce, turning to the Bible offers a unique perspective. The Bible is not just a religious text but a compendium of moral and ethical guidance that has shaped human thought and behavior for centuries. Its narratives are more than historical accounts; they are life lessons distilled into stories that transcend time and culture. From the Proverbs' practical advice to the Psalms' expressions of deep emotion, the

Bible's teachings cover a spectrum of human experiences and offer actionable insights.

The stories within this book illustrate various aspects of life where biblical wisdom can be applied. They range from personal dilemmas and emotional struggles to professional decisions and interpersonal relationships. By drawing on these narratives, the book demonstrates how ancient wisdom can provide answers to contemporary problems, encouraging readers to reflect on their own lives and seek guidance through faith.

Stories of Wisdom and Guidance

1. The Lost Key

Emma's story is one of anxiety and resolution. Losing a crucial key left her distressed and unsure. Her grandmother's advice to read the Bible for peace became a transformative experience. As Emma immersed herself in the scriptures, she found solace and clarity. The verses she encountered reinforced the importance of trusting in God's guidance. Through reflection and prayer, she remembered where she had left the key, discovering that the act of seeking divine wisdom helped her regain her composure and solve her problem.

This story highlights how reading the Bible can offer peace and direction in moments of stress and confusion. It illustrates the calming effect of spiritual reflection and the practical outcomes that can arise from seeking divine guidance.

2. The Broken Vase

Tim's accidental destruction of a cherished family vase left him feeling guilty and troubled. Turning to the Bible, he found comfort in the story of King David's repentance. The narrative taught him about forgiveness—both from others and for oneself. By reflecting on David's experience, Tim learned the value of accepting mistakes and seeking forgiveness. This biblical lesson helped him reconcile his feelings and repair his relationship with his family, demonstrating how the Bible's teachings on forgiveness can heal emotional wounds and restore harmony.

3. The Argument

Sarah and her friend's argument was causing significant strain in their relationship. In search of wisdom, Sarah read Proverbs, which offered teachings on patience and understanding. The verses she read encouraged her to approach the situation with humility and empathy. By applying these principles, she was able to mend their friendship and resolve the conflict. This story underscores the Bible's practical advice on handling disagreements and fostering positive relationships.

4. The Decision

John faced a critical decision between two job offers, both promising different opportunities. Seeking guidance, he turned to the Bible and found inspiration in Solomon's request for wisdom. Solomon's example of seeking divine insight before making a decision guided John in aligning his choice with his values. This story illustrates how biblical narratives can provide clarity and confidence in making significant life choices.

5. The Neighbor's Help

Lily was troubled by a neighbor's constant complaints, leading her to seek a solution through the Bible. She found a passage about loving thy neighbor, which inspired her to respond with kindness and patience. The result was a remarkable improvement in their relationship. This story demonstrates how biblical teachings on love and compassion can transform difficult interactions and build stronger community ties.

6. The Long Journey

Paul's upcoming long journey filled him with apprehension. To find comfort and protection, he turned to Psalms, seeking divine guidance and reassurance. The verses provided him with strength and confidence for his trip. This narrative emphasizes the Bible's role in offering comfort and courage during challenging or uncertain times.

7. The New Start

Rebecca was beginning a new chapter in her life after a setback, feeling uncertain about her future. The story of Job's resilience inspired her as she read the Bible. Job's perseverance through hardship encouraged her to embrace her challenges with determination and hope. This story illustrates how biblical stories of resilience and recovery can offer encouragement and strength during personal trials.

8. The Disagreement

Tom and his siblings were at odds over a family decision. By reading the Bible together, they found wisdom in Proverbs about seeking counsel and achieving unity. This collective reflection helped them reach a consensus and resolve their disagreement. This story highlights the Bible's guidance on collaboration and decision-making within family dynamics.

9. The Lost Faith

Maria struggled with her faith and felt disconnected. Reading the story of the Prodigal Son reminded her of God's boundless love and forgiveness. This renewed her faith and provided hope. This story underscores the Bible's message of redemption and the importance of faith during times of spiritual doubt.

10. The Illness

James was battling illness and feeling despair. The story of Hezekiah's recovery from illness, as recounted in the Bible, offered him comfort and hope. The verses on God's healing power provided solace and strength. This narrative demonstrates how biblical accounts of healing can inspire faith and resilience during health crises.

11. The Financial Strain

Anna faced financial difficulties and was worried about her future. Reading biblical passages about God's provision taught her to trust in divine timing and make wise financial decisions. Her faith led her to find unexpected support and solutions. This story illustrates how biblical teachings on provision and trust can guide individuals through financial challenges.

12. The Difficult Task

Mark was overwhelmed by a challenging project at work. Inspired by Nehemiah's perseverance in rebuilding the wall, he found renewed determination and successfully completed his task. This story highlights the Bible's lessons on perseverance and diligence in overcoming professional obstacles.

13. The Broken Friendship

Julia's friendship was strained, and she sought to mend it by turning to the Bible. The teachings on reconciliation in Matthew guided her approach, leading to a strengthened bond with her friend. This story emphasizes the Bible's wisdom on restoring and maintaining healthy relationships.

Conclusion

"Wisdom in the Word: Life Lessons from Biblical Stories" serves as a testament to the enduring relevance of biblical teachings. The stories within this book demonstrate how the wisdom of the Bible can provide practical guidance, comfort, and inspiration in various aspects of life. By reflecting on these narratives, readers are encouraged to seek divine wisdom and apply it to their own experiences, finding hope, clarity, and direction in the timeless teachings of the Bible.

Anthony Savio Herminio da Piedade Fernandes

[MFS, M.Com (F&C), M.Com (Accountancy), MA (PS), SET, NET]

ACKNOWLEDGEMENTS

I extend my deepest gratitude to everyone whose contributions and support have made this book possible. First and foremost, I thank my family for their unwavering encouragement and understanding throughout this endeavor. Their belief in me and patience during countless hours of writing and research have been my anchor.

Special thanks to Lambert Academic Publishing and the editorial team for their professionalism, guidance, and commitment to bringing this project to fruition. Your expertise and attention to detail have shaped this book into a coherent and impactful exploration of ethical themes.

I am immensely grateful to the scholars whose insights and research have informed the content of this book. Your work serves as the foundation upon which these discussions are built.

Anthony Savio Herminio da Piedade Fernandes

[MFS, M.Com (F&C), M.Com (Accountancy), MA (PS), SET, NET]

A NOTE OF THANKS

Dear Readers,

As I pen down this note, I am filled with immense gratitude and appreciation for your support and engagement with this book, "Wisdom in the Word: Life Lessons from Biblical Stories." Your willingness to explore the profound teachings of the Bible through the stories and lessons contained within these pages is both inspiring and deeply meaningful.

Writing this book has been a journey of reflection, exploration, and discovery. Each story and lesson was crafted with the hope of offering clarity and encouragement, drawing upon the timeless wisdom of biblical teachings. It is my sincere hope that these narratives have resonated with you and provided valuable insights into navigating the complexities of life.

I want to express my heartfelt thanks to everyone who contributed to the creation of this book. To my family and friends, whose unwavering support and encouragement were the cornerstone of this project, I am eternally grateful. Your belief in this endeavor kept me motivated through the writing process.

A special thanks to the scholars, theologians, and spiritual guides whose insights and interpretations enriched the content of this book. Your expertise helped shape the narratives and ensured that the wisdom conveyed remains true to the essence of biblical teachings.

To my readers, your engagement with this book means more than words can express. Your openness to exploring the lessons from the Bible and applying them to your lives is a testament to the enduring power of these teachings. I am honored to have been a part of your journey and hope that the stories shared have offered you guidance, comfort, and inspiration.

May the wisdom found in these pages continue to illuminate your path and provide you with strength and clarity in all your endeavors. Thank you once again for your support and for allowing me to share this journey with you.

With heartfelt appreciation,

Anthony Savio Herminio da Piedade Fernandes
[MFS, M.Com (F&C), M.Com (Accountancy), MA (PS), SET, NET]

ABOUT THE AUTHOR

 **Anthony Savio Herminio da Piedade Fernandes**

[MFS, M.Com (F&C), M.Com (Accountancy), MA (PS), SET, NET]

He is an educationist, a researcher, as well as a poet. His educational experience includes participating in and completing over 300 webinars/workshops and more than 300 certificate programs. Moreover, he has received multiple NPTEL certifications from IIT Madras, IIT Kharagpur, IIT Bombay, IIT Hyderabad, IIT Guwahati, IIT Kanpur, IIT Mandi, among other institutes. In addition to receiving various NPTEL Star Awards / Appreciations, he has also been awarded Domain Scholar three times in the fields of Economics & Finance, Marketing, and Patent & IPR. A few of the certificate courses he has taken have been offered by IIM Bangalore and other top higher education institutions in India. In the past few years, he has helped a large number of students clear NET / SET Exams in Commerce & Management subjects with success.

There are over 50 book chapters that he has contributed to national and international ISBN edited books and he has published two research papers in two international journals. Also, he held the position of Editor, Co-editor and Reviewer in some national and international ISBN edited books with various responsibilities. Furthermore, he holds over 50 patents and design publications under his belt. His other interest is poetry, and he has had some of his poems published over the years. Throughout his career, he has received many Awards/Appreciations for his outstanding contributions to educational and research publications.

Having founded "Trading Equations" to provide training in NSE Stock Market and MCX Commodity Market trading, he has been able to provide these services for free. As such, he has accumulated 16 NCFM Certificates leading to NCMP Level 5 in addition to his MCCP certification as well.

Furthermore, he is also passionate about organic farming. Philu's Farm is an organic farm initiative launched by him, in which he is a Co-Founder. In addition to his love of nature, he also loves animals.

He has studied Naturopathy, Yoga, etc and has successfully been able to cure some ailments. He has also done Diploma in Theology and other courses relating to Biblical Studies, etc.

"Investment in Education is the Best Investment"

– Anthony Savio Herminio da Piedade Fernandes

TABLE OF CONTENTS

CHAPTER 1

THE LOST KEY

Emma was known for her meticulous nature, but even the most organized individuals can have moments of oversight. One sunny afternoon, she realized that she had misplaced the key to her office—a crucial item that she needed for an important meeting. As the hours ticked away, her anxiety grew. She retraced her steps, checked every corner of her house, and even called her colleagues, hoping that someone might have seen or picked up the key. Despite her best efforts, the key remained elusive.

Feeling defeated and overwhelmed, Emma decided to take a break. She sat down in her favorite armchair and looked around for some comfort. Her gaze fell upon her Bible, which had been her companion through many of life's ups and downs. She had always found solace in its verses, so she decided to turn to it for some peace of mind.

Emma opened the Bible at random and began to read. The words of Psalm 119:105 caught her attention: "Your word is a lamp to my feet and a light for my path." She found comfort in this verse, feeling a sense of calm wash over her. She realized that this verse wasn't just about physical light but also about spiritual guidance. She prayed for clarity and asked for help in finding the lost key.

She continued reading and came across Proverbs 3:5-6: "Trust in the Lord with all your heart and lean not on your own understanding; in all your ways submit to him, and he will make your paths straight." The verses reminded her that, despite her best efforts, there were limits to what she could achieve on her own. She needed to trust in something greater than herself to find a solution.

Feeling reassured by the verses, Emma decided to take a different approach. Instead of continuing her frantic search, she took a moment to sit in silence and reflect on the situation. The Bible had provided her with a renewed sense of calm and perspective. Emma remembered that when she was reading earlier, she had been flipping through some old documents in her office. She recalled that the last time she saw the key, she had been sorting through a stack of papers and had placed the key somewhere safe but out of her usual sight.

With this new insight, Emma headed back to her office and focused her attention on the area where she had been sorting documents. As she carefully examined the space, she noticed a small drawer that she hadn't checked thoroughly before. Opening the drawer, she found the lost key tucked away among the papers. A wave of relief and gratitude washed over her.

Emma realized that the Bible had provided more than just comfort; it had given her practical wisdom. By finding calm and perspective through Scripture, she was able to approach the problem with a clearer mind and eventually locate the key. The experience reinforced her belief in the power of turning to spiritual guidance in moments of difficulty.

Reflection and Lessons Learned

Emma's experience with the lost key offers several lessons on the importance of seeking wisdom and comfort from the Bible in everyday life:

1. Spiritual Guidance in Times of Stress: When faced with a stressful situation, turning to the Bible can provide spiritual guidance that helps alleviate anxiety. The verses Emma read reminded her that even in

seemingly small problems, there is value in seeking divine support and guidance.

2. Trust in Divine Wisdom: The verses from Proverbs highlighted the importance of trusting in divine wisdom rather than solely relying on one's own understanding. Emma's trust in the Bible's teachings helped her approach the problem with a renewed perspective, ultimately leading her to the solution.

3. Calm and Reflection: Sometimes, taking a step back and reflecting on a problem with a calm mind can lead to solutions that were previously overlooked. Emma's moment of calmness, inspired by her Bible reading, allowed her to think more clearly and remember where she might have placed the key.

4. Practical Wisdom: The Bible's teachings are not only spiritually enriching but also offer practical wisdom that can be applied to everyday situations. Emma's experience showed that biblical principles can guide us in making thoughtful decisions and finding solutions to practical problems.

5. Connection Between Faith and Action: Emma's story illustrates the connection between faith and action. By integrating her faith with practical efforts, such as searching for the key, she was able to achieve a successful outcome. The Bible's teachings inspired her actions and provided her with a sense of purpose and direction.

6. The Power of Prayer: Emma's prayer for guidance was an important part of her experience. It exemplifies how prayer can be a powerful tool for seeking clarity and support in difficult situations. The act of praying helped Emma to focus her thoughts and trust in a higher power for assistance.

7. Embracing Spiritual Resources: The Bible, as a spiritual resource, offers comfort, guidance, and wisdom in various aspects of life. Emma's use of

the Bible during her time of need highlights its role as a source of strength and clarity.

The Broader Impact

Emma's story reflects a broader truth about the role of faith and spirituality in addressing life's challenges. For many individuals, the Bible serves as a source of comfort and guidance, offering wisdom that transcends immediate concerns. The experience also emphasizes the importance of integrating spiritual practices with practical efforts in order to navigate life's complexities.

In moments of difficulty, whether they are minor inconveniences or significant challenges, turning to spiritual resources can provide not only solace but also practical insights that can lead to solutions. The Bible's teachings encourage individuals to seek divine guidance, trust in a higher purpose, and approach problems with a sense of calm and perspective.

Furthermore, Emma's experience underscores the value of personal reflection and the power of combining faith with action. By reflecting on her situation through the lens of biblical wisdom, she was able to approach the problem with a clearer mind and ultimately find the lost key.

Conclusion

Emma's story about losing the key and finding it through biblical guidance illustrates the profound impact that faith and spirituality can have on everyday life. The Bible provided her with comfort, wisdom, and a renewed perspective, leading her to successfully resolve the problem. Her experience highlights the importance of seeking divine guidance, trusting in a higher purpose, and integrating spiritual insights with practical efforts. The story serves as a reminder of the valuable role that faith can play in addressing life's challenges and finding solutions to everyday problems.

CHAPTER 2

THE BROKEN VASE: A LESSON IN FORGIVENESS AND WISDOM

In a quaint, bustling town lived a young woman named Tim, who was renowned for her caring nature and meticulous attention to detail. Tim's home was filled with cherished items, each holding sentimental value. Among them was a delicate, antique vase passed down through generations. It was not just a decorative piece but a symbol of family heritage and love.

One afternoon, while Tim was cleaning her living room, she accidentally knocked the vase off a high shelf. The sound of shattering porcelain filled the room, and her heart sank. As she looked at the broken pieces scattered across the floor, she felt a pang of guilt and sorrow. The vase was irreplaceable, and its loss was a blow to her cherished family memories.

Overwhelmed with remorse, Tim found herself at a loss. She couldn't undo what had happened, and the weight of her mistake left her feeling despondent. She decided to seek solace and wisdom in her Bible, hoping to find some comfort and guidance through this emotional turmoil.

Seeking Comfort in the Bible

Tim picked up her Bible, hoping it would offer her some relief. She flipped through the pages, searching for a verse that might help her cope with the guilt she felt. As she read, she came across the story of King David and his repentance. The story touched her deeply and provided her with a new perspective on her situation.

In the story, King David had committed a grave error, but he sought forgiveness from God with a humble and contrite heart. His repentance was genuine, and he asked for mercy. Tim realized that her mistake, though significant, was not beyond redemption. This story of forgiveness resonated with her, and she found solace in the idea that she too could seek forgiveness, not just from others but from herself.

Tim also came across passages in Proverbs that spoke about wisdom and understanding. Proverbs 3:5-6, "Trust in the Lord with all your heart and lean not on your own understanding; in all your ways submit to him, and he will make your paths straight," offered her comfort. It reminded her that she didn't have to rely solely on her own strength and understanding. By trusting in a higher power, she could find a way through her difficulties.

Reflecting on Forgiveness

The Bible's teachings on forgiveness and repentance were instrumental in Tim's journey to healing. She realized that while the vase was precious, the true value lay in the lessons she could learn from the experience. She needed to forgive herself for the accident and not let guilt consume her.

Forgiveness was not just about asking for or granting it to others; it was also about accepting it for oneself. Tim recognized that being too hard on herself would not change the past but would only add to her distress. Embracing self-forgiveness allowed her to move forward with a sense of peace.

Rebuilding and Moving Forward

Tim understood that while she couldn't repair the vase, she could honor its memory by cherishing the lessons it had taught her. She decided to focus on what she could control: her actions and her attitude moving forward.

Inspired by her reflections, Tim reached out to her family to share her feelings and the lessons she had learned from the incident. Her family, though saddened by the loss of the vase, appreciated her honesty and the wisdom she had gained. They supported her in her journey of self-forgiveness and offered their understanding.

In the spirit of renewal, Tim used the experience as an opportunity to create new family traditions. She organized a family gathering where they shared stories of their ancestors and the values that the vase represented. Through these gatherings, the vase's legacy continued, albeit in a new form.

Lessons Learned

The story of the broken vase offers several valuable lessons about dealing with mistakes, seeking forgiveness, and finding wisdom:

1. The Importance of Self-Forgiveness: Tim's journey illustrates the necessity of forgiving oneself for mistakes. Guilt can be overwhelming, but it's important to recognize that everyone makes errors. Accepting self-forgiveness allows individuals to move past their mistakes and focus on personal growth.

2. Seeking Divine Guidance: Turning to spiritual texts for guidance during difficult times can provide comfort and perspective. The Bible's teachings helped Tim understand the value of forgiveness and trust in a higher power. This perspective can be a source of strength and clarity.

3. The Power of Repentance: The story of King David highlights the importance of sincere repentance. Acknowledging one's mistakes and seeking forgiveness can be a powerful step towards healing and personal development. It's not just about apologizing but also about making amends and learning from the experience.

4. Turning Challenges into Opportunities: While the loss of the vase was a significant blow, Tim's response demonstrates how challenges can be transformed into opportunities for growth. By focusing on what she could control and embracing new traditions, she honored the vase's memory and created positive outcomes from a difficult situation.

5. The Value of Family Support: Sharing one's struggles with family and loved ones can provide emotional support and strengthen relationships. Tim's openness about her feelings and the lessons she learned brought her closer to her family and helped them navigate the situation together.

6. Finding Wisdom in Adversity: Adversity often brings valuable lessons that may not be immediately apparent. Tim's experience with the broken vase taught her about forgiveness, self-compassion, and resilience. These lessons extended beyond the incident and enriched her overall perspective on life.

7. The Role of Spiritual Reflection: Reflecting on spiritual teachings during challenging times can offer new insights and help individuals find meaning in their experiences. Tim's engagement with the Bible provided her with a framework for understanding and coping with her emotions.

Conclusion

Tim's experience with the broken vase serves as a poignant reminder of the transformative power of forgiveness and wisdom. Through her journey of seeking comfort in the Bible, she learned valuable lessons about self-forgiveness, repentance, and the ability to turn challenges into opportunities for growth.

The story emphasizes the importance of trusting in a higher power, seeking guidance, and finding strength in spiritual teachings. It also highlights the value of sharing one's struggles with loved ones and using adversity as a catalyst for personal development.

In the end, while the vase could not be repaired, the wisdom and growth that emerged from the experience became a treasured part of Tim's journey. The lessons learned from the broken vase continued to shape her perspective, guiding her through future challenges with renewed strength and understanding.

CHAPTER 3

THE ARGUMENT: A JOURNEY TO UNDERSTANDING THROUGH BIBLICAL WISDOM

In a bustling town, two lifelong friends, Anna and Michael, found their relationship tested by a heated argument. Anna, a passionate advocate for social justice, had always been outspoken about her beliefs and was deeply involved in various causes. Michael, on the other hand, was more reserved and preferred to engage in discussions with a focus on practical solutions rather than ideological debates.

The argument began over a discussion about a recent social issue. Anna expressed her frustration with the slow pace of change and criticized some of Michael's views, which she felt were not progressive enough. Michael, feeling misunderstood and cornered, responded defensively, leading to a prolonged and bitter exchange. Their disagreement escalated to the point where both friends felt hurt and disrespected. The argument left them both feeling distant and estranged, questioning the strength and depth of their friendship.

Anna and Michael's argument not only strained their relationship but also left them both feeling emotionally drained and confused. In the midst of their frustration, Anna decided to seek guidance and clarity from her Bible. She hoped to find wisdom that could help her understand the nature of conflict, forgiveness, and how to restore her friendship with Michael.

Seeking Wisdom in Scripture

Anna turned to her Bible, hoping to find verses that might offer insight into her situation. She began reading passages that addressed conflict resolution, forgiveness, and the nature of friendship. One verse that particularly resonated with her was Proverbs 15:1: "A gentle answer turns away wrath, but a harsh word stirs up anger." This verse reminded Anna of the importance of approaching conflicts with a calm and considerate demeanor rather than escalating the situation with harsh words.

As she continued reading, Anna came across Matthew 18:15-17, which provides guidance on addressing grievances within the Christian community. It suggests a process for resolving conflicts by first addressing the issue directly with the person involved, then seeking mediation if necessary, and finally involving the community if the issue remains unresolved. This passage offered Anna a structured approach to reconciling with Michael, emphasizing direct communication and mutual understanding.

Another verse that stood out to Anna was Ephesians 4:32: "Be kind and compassionate to one another, forgiving each other, just as in Christ God forgave you." This verse underscored the importance of forgiveness and compassion in relationships. It reminded Anna that, just as she sought forgiveness from God, she needed to extend the same grace to Michael.

Reflecting on the Argument

With these verses in mind, Anna began to reflect on the nature of the argument and her role in it. She realized that her passion for social justice had led her to speak harshly and criticize Michael's views without fully understanding his perspective. She recognized that her approach had contributed to the escalation of the argument and that she needed to take responsibility for her part in the conflict.

Anna also considered Michael's position. She realized that while he might not have shared her enthusiasm for certain causes, his views were shaped by his own experiences and values. She understood that respecting his perspective and engaging in a more empathetic dialogue could help bridge the gap between them.

Reaching Out and Restoring the Relationship
Armed with a new perspective, Anna decided to reach out to Michael. She initiated a conversation with him, expressing her desire to resolve their differences and restore their friendship. She approached the conversation with humility and a willingness to listen, using the principles she had gleaned from her Bible reading.

Anna began the conversation by acknowledging her part in the argument and apologizing for any hurtful comments she had made. She expressed her genuine desire to understand Michael's perspective and to find common ground. Michael, initially hesitant, appreciated Anna's sincerity and willingness to engage in a respectful dialogue.

As they talked, Anna and Michael revisited the issues that had caused their disagreement. They both made an effort to listen actively and to express their viewpoints with empathy and understanding. They discovered that, despite their differing perspectives, they shared common values and goals. This realization helped them find common ground and work towards a resolution.

Through their conversation, Anna and Michael were able to address the underlying issues that had led to the argument. They discussed their expectations and boundaries, and they agreed to approach future disagreements with a focus on mutual respect and understanding. Their willingness to forgive each other and to work through their differences strengthened their friendship and helped them rebuild their connection.

Lessons Learned

The argument between Anna and Michael and their subsequent reconciliation offer several important lessons about conflict resolution, forgiveness, and the role of biblical wisdom in relationships:

1. The Importance of Gentle Communication: Proverbs 15:1 highlights the impact of communication style on conflict resolution. A gentle and considerate approach can help de-escalate tensions and foster understanding. Anna's realization of this principle helped her address the conflict with Michael more effectively.

2. Structured Conflict Resolution: Matthew 18:15-17 provides a structured approach to resolving conflicts within a community. By addressing grievances directly, seeking mediation, and involving others if necessary, individuals can work towards resolution in a systematic and respectful manner.

3. The Power of Forgiveness: Ephesians 4:32 emphasizes the importance of forgiveness in relationships. Extending grace and compassion to others, as God does with individuals, can help mend relationships and foster a spirit of reconciliation.

4. Self-Reflection and Accountability: Reflecting on one's role in a conflict and taking responsibility for one's actions are crucial steps in resolving disagreements. Anna's willingness to acknowledge her part in the

argument and to apologize for her behavior was a key factor in restoring her friendship with Michael.

5. Empathy and Understanding: Engaging in empathetic dialogue and making an effort to understand the other person's perspective can help bridge gaps and find common ground. Anna and Michael's ability to listen actively and respect each other's viewpoints played a significant role in their reconciliation.

6. Restoring Relationships Through Dialogue: Open and honest communication is essential for resolving conflicts and restoring relationships. By addressing the issues directly and engaging in a respectful conversation, Anna and Michael were able to rebuild their friendship and strengthen their bond.

7. Integrating Spiritual Wisdom into Everyday Life: The principles found in the Bible can provide valuable guidance for navigating conflicts and relationships. Integrating spiritual teachings into daily interactions can help individuals approach challenges with a sense of purpose and wisdom.

Broader Implications

The lessons from Anna and Michael's experience extend beyond their specific situation and offer broader insights into conflict resolution and relationship management. In various aspects of life, whether in personal relationships, professional settings, or community interactions, the principles of gentle communication, forgiveness, and empathy can help foster positive and respectful interactions.

Furthermore, integrating spiritual wisdom into everyday life can provide individuals with a sense of direction and purpose when facing challenges. The Bible's teachings on conflict resolution and forgiveness offer practical guidance for navigating interpersonal dynamics and building strong, supportive relationships.

In a world where conflicts and disagreements are inevitable, the ability to approach them with grace, understanding, and a willingness to seek resolution can make a significant difference. The principles of forgiveness, empathy, and respectful communication can help individuals navigate conflicts more effectively and build stronger connections with others.

Conclusion

The argument between Anna and Michael and their subsequent reconciliation serves as a powerful example of how biblical wisdom can guide individuals through conflicts and restore relationships. Through gentle communication, structured conflict resolution, and a focus on forgiveness and empathy, they were able to address their differences and rebuild their friendship.

The story underscores the importance of integrating spiritual teachings into everyday interactions and highlights the value of approaching conflicts with humility, understanding, and a willingness to listen. By applying these principles, individuals can navigate disagreements more effectively and foster stronger, more supportive relationships.

In the end, the experience not only strengthened Anna and Michael's friendship but also provided them with valuable lessons that would guide them in their future interactions. The journey from conflict to reconciliation serves as a testament to the transformative power of forgiveness, empathy, and spiritual wisdom in fostering meaningful and lasting connections.

CHAPTER 4

THE DECISION: CHOOSING FORGIVENESS THROUGH BIBLICAL WISDOM

In a vibrant community, there lived two individuals, Sarah and John, whose paths crossed frequently due to their involvement in local charitable activities. Sarah, a dedicated volunteer, and John, a prominent community leader, had collaborated on numerous projects aimed at improving the lives of those in need. Their shared commitment to helping others had fostered a strong working relationship and mutual respect.

However, a disagreement arose between them that threatened to undermine their partnership. Sarah had proposed a new initiative to address a pressing issue in the community, while John, concerned about the feasibility and impact, voiced strong objections. The discussion quickly escalated into a heated argument, with both parties becoming entrenched in their positions. The conflict reached a point where it not only affected their professional collaboration but also strained their personal relationship.

Sarah felt deeply hurt and disrespected by John's dismissal of her ideas and perceived lack of support. Similarly, John felt frustrated by Sarah's unwillingness to consider his concerns and perceived criticism of his leadership. Both were left with a choice: to continue harboring resentment and let the conflict fester or to seek resolution and rebuild their relationship.

Sarah, grappling with the emotional aftermath of the disagreement, turned to her Bible for solace and wisdom. She hoped to find guidance on how to approach the situation with a spirit of forgiveness and understanding.

One of the first passages that Sarah came across was Matthew 5:9: "Blessed are the peacemakers, for they shall be called children of God." This verse spoke to Sarah about the value of seeking peace and reconciliation. It reminded her that pursuing harmony in relationships was not only a noble endeavor but also aligned with her faith.

Sarah also found solace in Ephesians 4:31-32, which reads: "Get rid of all bitterness, rage and anger, brawling and slander, along with every form of malice. Be kind and compassionate to one another, forgiving each other, just as in Christ God forgave you." This passage highlighted the importance of letting go of negative emotions and embracing forgiveness. It encouraged Sarah to consider how she could extend grace to John, just as she hoped for grace in return.

Another key verse Sarah encountered was Proverbs 15:1: "A gentle answer turns away wrath, but a harsh word stirs up anger." This verse underscored the power of communication in resolving conflicts. Sarah realized that her approach to the disagreement had played a role in escalating the situation and that a more gentle and thoughtful response could help de-escalate tensions.

Reflecting on the Conflict
With these verses in mind, Sarah began to reflect on the nature of the conflict with John. She considered her own actions and responses during the

disagreement and recognized that her frustration and defensiveness had contributed to the escalation. Sarah acknowledged that while her passion for the initiative was genuine, her approach may have inadvertently alienated John.

Sarah also thought about John's perspective. She realized that his objections were rooted in genuine concerns for the community's well-being and the feasibility of the proposed initiative. Understanding this helped her appreciate that his stance was not a personal attack but rather a reflection of his commitment to responsible leadership.

Reaching Out and Seeking Reconciliation

Determined to restore their relationship, Sarah decided to reach out to John. She approached him with a genuine desire to resolve their differences and rebuild their partnership. Sarah began the conversation by acknowledging her part in the conflict and apologizing for any hurtful comments she had made. She expressed her appreciation for John's dedication to the community and his commitment to thoughtful decision-making.

John, initially reserved, appreciated Sarah's willingness to engage in a respectful dialogue. He acknowledged his own role in the conflict and expressed his commitment to finding a solution that would benefit the community. The conversation, grounded in mutual respect and understanding, marked the beginning of a process of healing and reconciliation.

During their discussion, Sarah and John revisited the issues that had led to their disagreement. They explored potential solutions and compromises that would address both their concerns and the needs of the community. Through open and honest communication, they were able to find common ground and develop a revised plan that incorporated elements of both their ideas.

The process of reconciliation also involved setting new expectations for their collaboration. Sarah and John agreed to approach future disagreements with a focus on constructive dialogue and mutual respect. They established clear communication channels and committed to addressing conflicts early on to prevent misunderstandings from escalating.

Lessons Learned

The journey of Sarah and John's reconciliation offers several important lessons about forgiveness, conflict resolution, and the role of biblical wisdom in relationships:

1. The Value of Peacemaking: Matthew 5:9 highlights the importance of seeking peace in relationships. By striving to be a peacemaker, individuals can foster harmony and strengthen their connections with others. Sarah's decision to pursue reconciliation with John exemplifies the value of this principle.

2. The Power of Forgiveness: Ephesians 4:31-32 emphasizes the importance of letting go of negative emotions and embracing forgiveness. Forgiveness is not only about releasing resentment but also about extending grace to others and fostering positive relationships.

3. The Role of Gentle Communication: Proverbs 15:1 underscores the impact of communication style on conflict resolution. A gentle and considerate approach can help de-escalate tensions and facilitate constructive dialogue. Sarah's realization of this principle helped her engage with John in a more effective manner.

4. Self-Reflection and Accountability: Reflecting on one's actions and taking responsibility for one's role in a conflict are crucial steps in resolving disagreements. Sarah's willingness to acknowledge her part in

the argument and to apologize for her behavior was a key factor in restoring her relationship with John.

5. Empathy and Understanding: Understanding the other person's perspective and appreciating their concerns can help bridge gaps and find common ground. Sarah's recognition of John's genuine concerns and commitment to the community played a significant role in their reconciliation.

6. Constructive Dialogue and Compromise: Open and honest communication, combined with a willingness to compromise, is essential for resolving conflicts and finding mutually beneficial solutions. Sarah and John's ability to discuss their differences and develop a revised plan demonstrates the effectiveness of this approach.

7. Setting Expectations for Future Interactions: Establishing clear expectations for communication and conflict resolution can help prevent misunderstandings and promote positive interactions. Sarah and John's commitment to addressing conflicts early and with mutual respect reflects this principle.

Broader Implications

The lessons from Sarah and John's experience extend beyond their specific situation and offer broader insights into conflict resolution and relationship management. In various contexts, whether in personal relationships, professional settings, or community interactions, the principles of forgiveness, empathy, and constructive communication can help foster positive and respectful interactions.

Integrating biblical wisdom into everyday interactions can provide individuals with a sense of direction and purpose when navigating conflicts. The teachings on peacemaking, forgiveness, and gentle communication offer practical guidance for managing disagreements and building strong, supportive relationships.

In a world where conflicts and disagreements are inevitable, the ability to approach them with grace, understanding, and a willingness to seek resolution can make a significant difference. By applying these principles, individuals can navigate conflicts more effectively and build stronger connections with others.

Conclusion

The decision of Sarah and John to seek reconciliation and restore their relationship serves as a powerful example of how biblical wisdom can guide individuals through conflicts and foster positive relationships. Through peacemaking, forgiveness, and constructive dialogue, they were able to address their differences and rebuild their partnership.

The story highlights the importance of integrating spiritual teachings into everyday interactions and underscores the value of approaching conflicts with humility, empathy, and a commitment to understanding. By applying these principles, individuals can navigate disagreements more effectively and cultivate meaningful and lasting connections with others.

In the end, the journey from conflict to reconciliation not only strengthened Sarah and John's relationship but also provided them with valuable lessons that would guide them in their future interactions. The decision to embrace forgiveness and seek peace serves as a testament to the transformative power of biblical wisdom in fostering meaningful and supportive relationships.

CHAPTER 5

THE NEIGHBOR'S HELP: A STORY OF WISDOM AND COMPASSION

In a quaint village nestled between rolling hills and lush fields, the bonds between neighbors were strong and woven with threads of mutual respect and care. The village was a place where people looked out for one another, and the community thrived on a spirit of cooperation and support. In this village lived Emily and her neighbor, Mr. Thompson. Emily was a young woman known for her kindness and generosity, while Mr. Thompson was an elderly widower who had lived alone since the passing of his wife several years ago.

Their relationship was friendly but distant. Emily admired Mr. Thompson for his wisdom and experience, but their interactions were mostly limited to polite greetings and occasional small talk. However, this was about to change in a way that would profoundly affect both of their lives.

The Challenge

One winter, the village experienced an unusually harsh storm. The snow piled high, and the temperatures plummeted. The storm was relentless, and the village found itself buried under a thick blanket of snow. The roads were impassable, and the cold made it dangerous to venture outside. The village was cut off from the outside world, and the residents had to rely on their own resources and each other for survival.

Emily, living in a cozy house with a well-stocked pantry, was prepared for the storm. She had stocked up on essentials and had a fireplace to keep warm.

However, she soon learned that Mr. Thompson's situation was different. His old house, though charming, was not as well-equipped for the harsh winter conditions. The storm had caused a power outage, leaving him without heat and electricity. His pantry was running low, and the isolation was taking a toll on his well-being.

Emily was concerned for Mr. Thompson's safety. She knew that the elderly were particularly vulnerable in such conditions, and she was determined to help him despite the challenging weather.

The Act of Kindness

Despite the storm's intensity, Emily decided to brave the elements to check on Mr. Thompson. She bundled up in warm clothing, secured her boots, and prepared herself for the arduous journey across the snow-covered streets. The wind howled and the snow whipped around her, but Emily was resolute in her mission.

When she arrived at Mr. Thompson's doorstep, she found him shivering and visibly distressed. His face lit up with relief when he saw Emily. She immediately offered him some of the supplies she had brought, including blankets, food, and firewood. Emily also checked the fireplace and ensured that it was properly set up to provide warmth.

Emily's presence was a source of immense comfort to Mr. Thompson. He expressed his gratitude, but Emily insisted that it was the least she could do for someone who had always been a good neighbor. She stayed with him for a while, sharing stories and ensuring that he was comfortable. Her compassion and willingness to help in such dire circumstances spoke volumes about her character.

Reflecting on Biblical Wisdom

In the midst of their interaction, Emily found herself reflecting on biblical teachings that emphasized the importance of compassion and neighborly love. The story of the Good Samaritan from the Bible came to mind. In the parable, a Samaritan helps a man who has been attacked and left for dead, demonstrating that true compassion knows no boundaries. This parable resonated deeply with Emily's actions, as she had reached out to help someone in need, regardless of their past interactions or differences.

Another verse that came to mind was Galatians 6:2: "Carry each other's burdens, and in this way, you will fulfill the law of Christ." Emily's decision to assist Mr. Thompson in his time of need was a practical application of this principle. By helping him through a difficult situation, she was embodying the spirit of this biblical teaching.

Emily also considered the verse from 1 John 3:17: "If anyone has material possessions and sees a brother or sister in need but has no pity on them, how can the love of God be in that person?" This verse highlighted the importance of not just having resources but also using them to make a difference in others' lives. Emily's actions were a reflection of her love and concern for Mr. Thompson, demonstrating how the love of God could manifest in practical acts of kindness.

The Impact of Emily's Help

Emily's assistance had a profound impact on Mr. Thompson. Not only did he receive the physical necessities needed to survive the storm, but he also experienced a renewed sense of community and connection. The storm had been a harsh reminder of the isolation that can come with aging and living alone, but Emily's visit reassured him that he was not forgotten.

Mr. Thompson, deeply moved by Emily's kindness, found himself reflecting on the nature of neighborly love and community. He realized that the bonds between neighbors were not just about friendly interactions but also about being there for each other in times of need. The storm had revealed the true strength of the village's sense of community, and Mr. Thompson felt a renewed appreciation for the people around him.

In the days following the storm, Emily continued to check on Mr. Thompson and ensured that he had everything he needed. The storm eventually passed, and life in the village returned to normal, but the experience left a lasting impression on both Emily and Mr. Thompson.

Lessons Learned

The story of Emily and Mr. Thompson offers several important lessons about kindness, community, and biblical wisdom:

1. The Importance of Compassion: Emily's actions exemplify the importance of compassion and neighborly love. Regardless of past interactions, she reached out to help Mr. Thompson in a time of need, demonstrating that true compassion involves putting others' needs before one's own.

2. Practical Application of Biblical Teachings: The story illustrates how biblical teachings can be applied in everyday situations. By helping Mr. Thompson, Emily embodied the principles of the Good Samaritan and the teachings from Galatians and 1 John, showing how faith can guide and inspire practical acts of kindness.

3. The Strength of Community Bonds: The storm revealed the strength of the village's sense of community. In times of crisis, the bonds between neighbors become even more significant, highlighting the importance of looking out for one another and supporting each other through difficult times.

4. The Impact of Simple Acts of Kindness: Emily's seemingly simple acts of kindness had a profound impact on Mr. Thompson. Her willingness to help not only provided him with the necessities for survival but also restored his sense of connection and community.

5. The Value of Selflessness: Emily's selfless decision to help Mr. Thompson, despite the harsh conditions, underscores the value of putting others' needs before one's own. It serves as a reminder that acts of kindness often require sacrifice and effort but are deeply rewarding.

6. Building Stronger Relationships: The experience of the storm strengthened the relationship between Emily and Mr. Thompson. Their newfound connection was a testament to the power of shared experiences and mutual support in building stronger, more meaningful relationships.

Broader Implications

The lessons from Emily and Mr. Thompson's story extend beyond their specific situation and offer broader insights into community dynamics and interpersonal relationships. The principles of compassion, neighborly love, and practical application of faith can be valuable in various contexts, including personal relationships, community involvement, and professional settings.

In personal relationships, practicing kindness and empathy can help resolve conflicts and build stronger connections. In community settings, supporting each other through challenges fosters a sense of solidarity and resilience. In professional environments, demonstrating compassion and understanding can enhance teamwork and collaboration.

By integrating biblical wisdom into everyday interactions, individuals can navigate challenges with a sense of purpose and integrity. The teachings on compassion, selflessness, and community support offer practical guidance for fostering positive and supportive relationships in all areas of life.

Conclusion

The story of Emily and Mr. Thompson serves as a powerful example of how biblical wisdom can guide individuals in their interactions with others. Through acts of kindness and compassion, Emily was able to help her neighbor in a time of need, demonstrating the practical application of biblical teachings on love and community.

The impact of Emily's help extended beyond the immediate relief she provided; it strengthened the bond between her and Mr. Thompson and highlighted the importance of neighborly love and support. The lessons learned from their experience offer valuable insights into the nature of compassion, the strength of community, and the role of faith in guiding practical actions.

In the end, the story of Emily and Mr. Thompson reminds us of the transformative power of kindness and the enduring value of supporting one another through life's challenges. By embracing these principles, individuals can cultivate meaningful relationships and contribute to the well-being of their communities.

CHAPTER 6

In a small, serene village surrounded by mountains and rivers, there lived a humble farmer named David. Known for his unwavering faith and dedication to his family and community, David led a life marked by hard work and simplicity. His farm, though modest, was a source of pride and sustenance for his family. However, David's life was about to be tested in ways he had never anticipated.

The Call to Adventure

One day, as David was tending to his fields, he received unexpected news from a distant relative. His uncle, a successful merchant, had fallen gravely ill and was in urgent need of assistance. David's uncle had been a source of support for the village in the past, and his illness was a matter of concern for many. The relative conveyed that David's presence was needed to help manage his uncle's affairs and provide comfort during his final days.

The journey to his uncle's estate was long and arduous, spanning hundreds of miles through rugged terrain and unpredictable weather. Despite the challenges, David felt a deep sense of responsibility and commitment to help his uncle in his time of need. He prepared for the journey, gathering supplies, saying goodbye to his family, and setting out with a heart full of determination and faith.

The Trials Along the Way

The journey proved to be far more difficult than David had anticipated. The path was fraught with obstacles: treacherous mountain passes, swollen rivers, and harsh weather conditions. David encountered numerous challenges, including getting lost in dense forests, dealing with severe storms, and facing exhaustion from the relentless travel. Each day brought new difficulties, testing his resolve and faith.

At one point, David's provisions began to run low, and he struggled to find food and shelter. He was tempted to abandon his quest and return home, but he remembered the importance of his mission and the need to support his ailing uncle. Despite his fatigue and discouragement, David pressed on, relying on his faith and perseverance to guide him through the hardships.

Moments of Reflection and Faith

During his journey, David found moments of reflection and spiritual renewal. In the quiet of the night, under the vast expanse of the stars, he would often find solace in prayer and meditation. He sought strength and guidance from his faith, asking for the endurance to complete his mission and the wisdom to navigate the trials he faced.

One particular night, as David rested by a small stream, he read from his Bible, finding comfort in passages that spoke to the themes of perseverance and divine support. He recalled the story of Job, who faced immense suffering yet remained steadfast in his faith. This story resonated deeply with David, offering him reassurance that even in the face of adversity, faith could provide strength and purpose.

He also drew inspiration from Philippians 4:13: "I can do all things through Christ who strengthens me." This verse became a source of motivation, reminding David that his journey, though challenging, was within the realm of possibility with divine assistance. It encouraged him to keep moving forward, even when the path seemed insurmountable.

The Arrival and the Impact

After enduring countless hardships, David finally reached his uncle's estate. The sight of the grand estate and the presence of his uncle, frail but grateful, brought a sense of relief and fulfillment. David's uncle, deeply touched by David's dedication and sacrifice, expressed his gratitude and admiration.

David's arrival not only provided much-needed assistance but also offered comfort and companionship to his uncle during his final days. The family was grateful for David's presence, and his actions served as a reminder of the importance of family bonds and support.

David's journey had a profound impact on his uncle's estate. His presence brought stability and hope during a difficult time, and his faith and perseverance inspired those around him. The story of David's journey became a testament to the power of commitment, faith, and resilience in the face of adversity.

Lessons Learned

David's long journey offers several valuable lessons about faith, perseverance, and the impact of personal sacrifice:

1. The Power of Perseverance: David's determination to complete his journey despite numerous obstacles highlights the importance of perseverance. His willingness to face challenges head-on and continue

moving forward, even when the path was difficult, underscores the value of persistence in achieving one's goals.

2. The Role of Faith in Overcoming Adversity: Throughout his journey, David relied on his faith to guide and sustain him. His spiritual reflections and prayers provided him with the strength to endure hardships and maintain his focus on the mission. This demonstrates how faith can play a crucial role in navigating difficult situations and finding purpose in challenges.

3. The Importance of Commitment and Sacrifice: David's decision to undertake the long journey despite the personal hardships illustrates the significance of commitment and sacrifice. His willingness to put the needs of his uncle and family before his own comfort highlights the value of selflessness and dedication to others.

4. The Impact of Personal Actions: David's actions had a significant impact on his uncle's estate and family. His presence provided comfort, stability, and inspiration during a difficult time. This emphasizes how individual actions, driven by compassion and faith, can have a profound effect on others and contribute to a greater sense of community and support.

5. Finding Strength in Spiritual Teachings: The story of David's journey reflects the relevance of spiritual teachings in providing guidance and strength. Biblical passages and stories, such as the story of Job and Philippians 4:13, offered David comfort and motivation. This highlights how spiritual teachings can offer practical support and encouragement in the face of challenges.

6. The Value of Reflection and Renewal: David's moments of reflection and prayer during his journey played a crucial role in sustaining his spirit and focus. The act of taking time for spiritual renewal and seeking guidance can be a powerful tool for maintaining resilience and navigating difficult situations.

Broader Implications

The lessons from David's journey extend beyond his specific situation and offer broader insights into personal growth, faith, and the impact of individual actions. The principles of perseverance, faith, and commitment can be applied in various contexts, including personal challenges, professional endeavors, and community involvement.

In personal life, embracing perseverance and faith can help individuals overcome obstacles and achieve their goals. In professional settings, the principles of commitment and sacrifice can drive success and foster a sense of purpose and dedication. In community contexts, personal actions driven by compassion and faith can contribute to the well-being and support of others.

By integrating spiritual teachings and values into everyday life, individuals can navigate challenges with greater resilience and purpose. The story of David's journey serves as a reminder of the transformative power of faith and perseverance in achieving meaningful outcomes and making a positive impact on others.

Conclusion

David's long journey is a powerful testament to the values of faith, perseverance, and personal sacrifice. His determination to help his ailing uncle despite the numerous obstacles he faced highlights the significance of commitment and resilience. The impact of his actions on his uncle's estate and family demonstrates the profound effect of individual contributions driven by compassion and faith.

The story also underscores the importance of finding strength and guidance in spiritual teachings. Biblical passages and reflections provided David with the motivation and reassurance needed to overcome challenges and maintain his focus on the mission.

Ultimately, David's journey serves as an inspiring example of how faith and perseverance can guide individuals through difficult times and lead to meaningful outcomes. By embracing these principles and applying them in various aspects of life, individuals can navigate challenges with greater resilience and contribute to the well-being of others. The lessons from David's journey offer valuable insights into the power of commitment, the role of faith, and the impact of personal actions in shaping a better world.

CHAPTER 7

THE NEW START: A JOURNEY OF TRANSFORMATION THROUGH FAITH

In a bustling city filled with the constant hum of activity, there lived a man named Thomas. A seasoned businessman, Thomas had built a successful career in finance. His days were filled with meetings, financial reports, and the relentless pursuit of profit. Despite his professional success, Thomas felt a growing sense of emptiness in his life. The demands of his career left him little time for personal reflection or spiritual growth. As he approached his mid-forties, Thomas began to question the purpose and direction of his life.

It was during this period of introspection that Thomas experienced a turning point. A series of events led him to reevaluate his priorities and seek a deeper meaning in life. This is the story of how Thomas embarked on a journey of transformation, guided by faith and the quest for a new start.

The Catalyst for Change

The catalyst for Thomas's transformation came unexpectedly. He had always been a person who relied on logic and reason, but a sudden health scare shook him to his core. During a routine check-up, Thomas's doctor informed him that he had high blood pressure and was at risk of serious health complications. The diagnosis served as a wake-up call, prompting Thomas to reassess his lifestyle and values.

In addition to his health scare, Thomas faced a personal crisis when his long-time mentor and friend, Mr. Williams, passed away. Mr. Williams had been a guiding force in Thomas's career, and his death left a void in Thomas's life. As he mourned the loss, Thomas found himself reflecting on the impact Mr. Williams had on him and the legacy he wished to leave behind.

These events acted as a catalyst for Thomas's journey towards change. He realized that his pursuit of material success had come at the expense of his well-being and personal fulfillment. This realization set him on a path to seek a new start, one that would bring greater meaning and purpose to his life.

The Search for Meaning

Thomas's search for meaning began with a quest for spiritual growth. Although he had been raised in a religious household, he had drifted away from his faith over the years. He decided to revisit his spiritual roots and explore ways to reconnect with his beliefs. Thomas started attending church services and participating in Bible study groups. He also began reading religious texts and reflecting on their teachings.

During his spiritual journey, Thomas encountered several biblical passages that resonated deeply with him. One passage that stood out was Matthew 6:33: "But seek first his kingdom and his righteousness, and all these things will be given to you as well." This verse spoke to Thomas's desire to realign his priorities and seek a higher purpose beyond material success.

Another verse that impacted Thomas was Jeremiah 29:11: "For I know the plans I have for you, declares the Lord, plans to prosper you and not to harm you, plans to give you hope and a future." This verse provided Thomas with reassurance that there was a divine plan for his life and that he could find hope and renewal through faith.

Thomas's spiritual exploration also led him to the parable of the Prodigal Son. The story of a young man who squandered his inheritance and later returned to his father's house seeking forgiveness resonated with Thomas's own sense of loss and desire for redemption. The parable reminded him that it was never too late to make a fresh start and seek forgiveness.

Embracing Change

As Thomas deepened his spiritual understanding, he began to make significant changes in his life. He realized that true fulfillment required more than just professional success; it involved nurturing relationships, contributing to the community, and living a life of purpose.

Thomas decided to simplify his life and prioritize what truly mattered to him. He reduced his work hours and focused on spending quality time with his family. He also engaged in volunteer work, offering his financial expertise to non-profit organizations and supporting causes that aligned with his values.

One of the key areas of transformation for Thomas was his approach to work. He had always been driven by the pursuit of profit, but he began to see his work as an opportunity to make a positive impact. He shifted his focus from purely financial gains to using his skills and resources to benefit others. This new perspective brought him a sense of fulfillment and satisfaction that he had never experienced before.

Thomas also made a conscious effort to cultivate gratitude and mindfulness in his daily life. He started keeping a journal to reflect on the blessings in his life and practice gratitude for the small and big things. This practice helped him stay grounded and appreciative of the present moment, rather than constantly striving for more.

The Role of Faith in Transformation

Thomas's journey of transformation was deeply intertwined with his faith. The spiritual insights and biblical teachings he encountered played a crucial role in guiding his decisions and shaping his new outlook on life.

Faith provided Thomas with a sense of purpose and direction. It helped him navigate the challenges and uncertainties of his journey with resilience and hope. The teachings of forgiveness, redemption, and renewal offered him a framework for understanding his own experiences and finding meaning in his struggles.

One of the most significant aspects of Thomas's faith journey was his renewed commitment to living a life of integrity and compassion. He began to see his actions through the lens of his faith, striving to align his behavior with the values of love, kindness, and humility.

Thomas also found solace in the support of his faith community. The connections he formed with fellow believers provided him with encouragement, accountability, and a sense of belonging. Sharing his journey with others who had similar experiences helped him stay motivated and inspired.

The Impact of the New Start

The changes Thomas made in his life had a profound impact on his well-being and overall sense of fulfillment. By prioritizing relationships, contributing to the community, and living with purpose, he experienced a renewed sense of joy and satisfaction.

Thomas's family also benefited from his transformation. The quality time he spent with them strengthened their bonds and created lasting memories. His decision to be more present and attentive brought his family closer together and fostered a supportive and loving environment.

In his professional life, Thomas's shift in perspective led to a more balanced approach to work. He continued to achieve success, but his focus on using his skills for the greater good brought a sense of fulfillment that went beyond financial gains. His colleagues and clients noticed the positive changes in his attitude, and he became known for his integrity and compassion.

Thomas's volunteer work also had a meaningful impact on the community. His financial expertise and dedication to supporting charitable causes made a difference in the lives of those he served. The sense of purpose he found through his volunteer efforts added a new dimension to his life and reinforced his commitment to making a positive impact.

Lessons Learned

Thomas's journey of transformation offers several valuable lessons about faith, personal growth, and the pursuit of a meaningful life:

1. The Importance of Self-Reflection: Thomas's journey began with a period of introspection and self-reflection. Taking the time to evaluate one's life and values can be a crucial step in identifying areas for growth and making positive changes.

2. The Role of Faith in Finding Purpose: Faith played a central role in Thomas's transformation. Spiritual teachings and biblical passages provided him with guidance, reassurance, and a sense of purpose. Faith can be a powerful tool for navigating life's challenges and finding meaning.

3. The Value of Prioritizing Relationships: By focusing on his family and relationships, Thomas experienced greater fulfillment and happiness. Prioritizing meaningful connections and spending quality time with loved ones can enhance overall well-being and create a supportive environment.

4. The Impact of Living with Purpose: Thomas's shift in focus from material success to living with purpose brought him a sense of fulfillment and satisfaction. Aligning one's actions with personal values and contributing to the greater good can lead to a more meaningful and rewarding life.

5. The Benefits of Gratitude and Mindfulness: Practicing gratitude and mindfulness helped Thomas stay grounded and appreciative of the present moment. These practices can enhance overall well-being and foster a positive outlook on life.

6. The Power of Community Support: Thomas's involvement in his faith community provided him with encouragement and a sense of belonging. Engaging with a supportive community can offer valuable resources, motivation, and connection.

Broader Implications

The lessons from Thomas's journey extend beyond his specific experiences and offer broader insights into personal growth, faith, and the pursuit of a meaningful life. The principles of self-reflection, faith, and purpose can be applied in various contexts, including personal development, professional endeavors, and community involvement.

In personal life, embracing self-reflection and faith can guide individuals in making meaningful changes and finding purpose. In professional settings, prioritizing relationships and living with purpose can lead to greater fulfillment and success. In community contexts, contributing to the greater good and engaging with a supportive network can create positive impact and connection. By integrating these principles into everyday life, individuals can navigate challenges with greater resilience and create a more meaningful and fulfilling existence. The story of Thomas's transformation serves as an inspiring example of how faith and personal growth can lead to a new start and a more purposeful life.

Conclusion

Thomas's journey of transformation is a powerful example of how faith, self-reflection, and purposeful living can lead to a new start and a more fulfilling life. His experiences highlight the importance of evaluating one's values, prioritizing relationships, and living with purpose. Through his renewed commitment to faith and his focus on making a positive impact, Thomas found greater meaning and satisfaction in his life.

The lessons from Thomas's story offer valuable insights into personal growth and the pursuit of a meaningful existence. By embracing these principles and applying them in various aspects of life, individuals can navigate challenges with resilience, find purpose, and create a positive impact on themselves and others. Thomas's journey serves as a reminder that it is never too late to make a fresh start and seek a life of greater fulfillment and purpose.

CHAPTER 8

THE DISAGREEMENT: A JOURNEY TOWARDS UNDERSTANDING THROUGH FAITH

In a picturesque town known for its vibrant community and picturesque landscapes, two longtime friends, Samuel and Jonathan, found themselves embroiled in a heated disagreement. Both were devout individuals who had shared countless discussions about faith, values, and their interpretations of religious teachings. However, a particular issue had arisen, challenging their friendship and prompting a journey of understanding and reconciliation. This is the story of how Samuel and Jonathan navigated their disagreement and discovered deeper truths about faith and friendship.

The Catalyst for Conflict

The disagreement between Samuel and Jonathan began over a theological debate that had been brewing for some time. Both men were active members of their church and had participated in various Bible study groups together. They held different perspectives on a particular doctrine, which led to an escalating disagreement. The issue in question was the interpretation of a specific biblical passage and its implications for their faith.

Samuel believed that the passage, which dealt with the concept of divine grace and salvation, implied a more inclusive and universal approach to salvation. He argued that God's grace was available to all people, regardless of their specific beliefs or actions. Jonathan, on the other hand, interpreted the passage as emphasizing the importance of adhering to specific religious practices and beliefs for salvation. He felt that faith required a more structured approach and adherence to established doctrines.

As the debate intensified, their discussions became more passionate and contentious. What started as a difference in interpretation evolved into a significant point of contention that threatened to strain their friendship. The disagreement was not only about theological perspectives but also about their personal convictions and how they understood their roles in their faith community.

The Emotional Toll

The emotional toll of the disagreement was considerable. Both Samuel and Jonathan valued their friendship deeply and had always respected each other's views, even when they differed. However, the intensity of the debate began to overshadow their mutual respect and affection. The discussions became heated, and both men found themselves feeling frustrated, misunderstood, and increasingly distant from each other.

Samuel felt disheartened by Jonathan's rigid stance and the perceived lack of openness to alternative perspectives. He struggled with the idea that his long-time friend could not see the validity of his interpretation. Jonathan, on the other hand, felt that Samuel's approach undermined the importance of doctrinal adherence and was concerned about the potential implications of a more inclusive interpretation.

Their conversations became strained, and they found it difficult to communicate effectively. The disagreement affected not only their interactions with each other but also their sense of peace and well-being. They both wondered if their friendship could survive the conflict and if they could find a way to reconcile their differences.

Seeking Guidance

Recognizing the impact of the disagreement on their friendship and personal peace, both Samuel and Jonathan decided to seek guidance. They turned to their pastor, Reverend Thomas, for support and perspective. Reverend Thomas was known for his wisdom and ability to offer insightful counsel on matters of faith and personal relationships.

Samuel and Jonathan scheduled separate meetings with Reverend Thomas to discuss their concerns and seek advice on how to approach the situation. During their meetings, they expressed their feelings, frustrations, and the impact of the disagreement on their relationship.

Reverend Thomas listened attentively and provided thoughtful guidance. He emphasized the importance of approaching disagreements with a spirit of humility and openness. He reminded them that differences in interpretation were common within religious communities and that respectful dialogue was crucial for maintaining unity and understanding.

Reverend Thomas also encouraged Samuel and Jonathan to reflect on their shared values and the core tenets of their faith. He reminded them that, despite their differences, they were united by their commitment to love, compassion, and the pursuit of spiritual growth.

The Path to Reconciliation

With Reverend Thomas's guidance, Samuel and Jonathan began to approach their disagreement with a renewed perspective. They recognized the need to move beyond the surface-level conflict and seek a deeper understanding of each other's viewpoints. They decided to engage in open and respectful dialogue, focusing on listening and empathizing with one another.

The process of reconciliation involved several key steps:
1. Active Listening: Samuel and Jonathan made a conscious effort to listen actively to each other's perspectives without interrupting or dismissing their views. They sought to understand the underlying reasons for each other's interpretations and the personal experiences that influenced their beliefs.
2. Expressing Vulnerability: Both men were willing to express their vulnerabilities and uncertainties. They shared their personal struggles and the impact of the disagreement on their faith and sense of belonging. This openness fostered a deeper connection and mutual empathy.
3. Finding Common Ground: Samuel and Jonathan identified areas of common ground in their beliefs. They acknowledged their shared commitment to their faith and the core values that united them. By focusing on these commonalities, they were able to build a foundation for understanding.
4. Respecting Differences: They agreed to respect each other's differences and recognize that diverse interpretations could coexist within their faith community. They understood that their disagreement did not diminish their friendship or their shared commitment to spiritual growth.
5. Forgiveness and Reconciliation: Both Samuel and Jonathan expressed forgiveness for any hurtful comments or actions during the disagreement. They acknowledged the impact of their words and committed to moving forward with a spirit of reconciliation and mutual respect.

The Transformation of Friendship

As Samuel and Jonathan worked through their disagreement, their friendship underwent a transformation. The process of reconciliation deepened their understanding of each other and strengthened their bond. They learned valuable lessons about the nature of faith, the importance of humility, and the value of open dialogue.

The disagreement also prompted both men to grow spiritually and personally. They gained a greater appreciation for the diversity of perspectives within their faith community and developed a more nuanced understanding of theological concepts. Their journey of reconciliation enhanced their ability to navigate future conflicts with grace and empathy.

Their renewed friendship became a source of inspiration for others in their faith community. Samuel and Jonathan shared their experiences and the lessons they had learned, encouraging others to approach disagreements with respect and a willingness to listen. Their story served as a reminder of the power of faith to heal and transform relationships.

Lessons Learned

The story of Samuel and Jonathan's disagreement offers several valuable lessons about faith, relationships, and the process of reconciliation:

1. The Importance of Humility: Approaching disagreements with humility and openness is crucial for maintaining respectful dialogue. Recognizing that one's perspective is not the only valid interpretation fosters a spirit of understanding and cooperation.

2. The Role of Active Listening: Active listening is essential for understanding different viewpoints and finding common ground.

Listening attentively and empathetically allows individuals to address the underlying issues and build meaningful connections.

3. The Value of Shared Values: Identifying and focusing on shared values can help bridge gaps between differing perspectives. Shared commitments and goals provide a foundation for unity and collaboration.

4. The Power of Forgiveness: Forgiveness is a key component of reconciliation. Acknowledging and addressing hurtful actions and comments allows individuals to move forward with renewed understanding and respect.

5. The Impact of Faith in Healing Relationships: Faith can play a significant role in healing and transforming relationships. The principles of love, compassion, and humility guide individuals towards resolution and deeper connections.

6. The Benefit of Seeking Guidance: Seeking guidance from trusted mentors or leaders can provide valuable perspective and support during times of conflict. Experienced counselors offer insights and strategies for navigating disagreements with grace and wisdom.

Broader Implications

The lessons from Samuel and Jonathan's disagreement extend beyond their specific situation and offer broader insights into the nature of conflict resolution and personal growth. The principles of humility, active listening, and shared values can be applied in various contexts, including personal relationships, professional settings, and community interactions.

In personal relationships, approaching conflicts with humility and empathy can foster deeper understanding and strengthen connections. In professional settings, effective communication and respect for diverse perspectives contribute to a positive and collaborative work environment. In community interactions, promoting dialogue and reconciliation helps build inclusive and supportive communities.

By integrating these principles into everyday life, individuals can navigate conflicts with greater resilience and create more meaningful and harmonious relationships. The story of Samuel and Jonathan serves as an inspiring example of how faith and mutual respect can guide individuals through disagreements and lead to personal and relational transformation.

Conclusion

The story of Samuel and Jonathan's disagreement is a compelling example of how faith, humility, and open dialogue can lead to reconciliation and personal growth. Their journey highlights the importance of approaching conflicts with respect, actively listening to different perspectives, and finding common ground. Through their process of reconciliation, they deepened their understanding of each other and strengthened their friendship.

The lessons learned from their experience offer valuable insights into navigating disagreements and fostering meaningful relationships. By embracing principles of humility, empathy, and forgiveness, individuals can address conflicts with grace and create a positive impact in their personal, professional, and community interactions. The story of Samuel and Jonathan serves as a reminder of the transformative power of faith and the potential for growth and healing through respectful dialogue and mutual understanding.

CHAPTER 9

THE LOST FAITH: A JOURNEY FROM DOUBT TO ENLIGHTENMENT

Faith is a delicate and profoundly personal aspect of human life. It can be a source of immense strength and comfort, yet it can also become a point of intense struggle and doubt. "The Lost Faith" is a story of a young woman named Emily who, after losing her faith, embarks on a transformative journey that leads her back to spiritual enlightenment. Her story is one of self-discovery, resilience, and the rediscovery of faith in a way that profoundly changes her life and perspective.

The Crisis of Faith

Emily grew up in a religious family where faith was an integral part of daily life. She attended church regularly, participated in youth groups, and was deeply involved in her community's religious activities. Her upbringing instilled in her a strong sense of belief and a clear understanding of her spiritual path. However, as she transitioned into adulthood, Emily began to encounter challenges that shook her faith to its core.

During her college years, Emily faced a series of personal and academic struggles. The pressures of academic life, coupled with a tumultuous relationship, left her feeling overwhelmed and disillusioned. She began questioning the very foundations of her beliefs. The teachings that once brought her comfort now seemed distant and irrelevant. Emily felt abandoned by a higher power and struggled to reconcile her suffering with the idea of a benevolent God.

The turning point came during a particularly difficult semester when Emily's academic performance suffered due to her emotional turmoil. She felt isolated and unsupported, and her previous convictions about faith and divine purpose seemed increasingly out of reach. This period of crisis led her to make a painful decision: she decided to step away from her faith, believing that it no longer served her or made sense in her current reality.

The Quest for Meaning

Emily's decision to distance herself from her faith led her on a quest for meaning. She explored various philosophies, self-help techniques, and spiritual practices, hoping to find something that would fill the void left by her lost faith. Her journey was marked by a search for purpose and understanding in a world that now seemed devoid of divine intervention.

She delved into the teachings of different religions and spiritual traditions, trying to find a new framework that resonated with her. Emily attended meditation retreats, read extensively about Eastern philosophies, and engaged in discussions with people of various beliefs. Despite her efforts, she struggled to find a sense of peace or connection.

One of the most profound experiences during this period was a trip to a remote Buddhist monastery. There, Emily immersed herself in meditation and mindfulness practices, hoping that these techniques might offer her solace and clarity. While she appreciated the tranquility and discipline of the monastic life, she found that it did not fully address the deep spiritual questions and doubts she grappled with.

Her quest for meaning also included a period of self-reflection and exploration of her personal values and goals. Emily began to question not only her beliefs but also her purpose in life. She evaluated her relationships, career aspirations, and personal aspirations, seeking a sense of direction and fulfillment. However, she still felt that something fundamental was missing.

The Encounter with a Wise Mentor

As Emily continued her search for meaning, she encountered a wise and compassionate mentor named Father Michael. Father Michael was a retired priest who had spent many years working with individuals struggling with their faith. He had a reputation for his deep understanding of both spiritual and existential issues and had a gift for guiding people through their crises of faith. Emily met Father Michael during a community outreach event. Despite her initial hesitation, she found herself drawn to his kindness and wisdom. They began a series of conversations that gradually helped Emily open up about her struggles and doubts. Father Michael listened attentively and offered thoughtful, non-judgmental responses. He did not attempt to force his beliefs on Emily but instead encouraged her to explore her questions and feelings deeply.

Through their conversations, Father Michael introduced Emily to the concept of faith as a journey rather than a destination. He emphasized that faith could be dynamic and evolving, and that doubts and struggles were a natural part of spiritual growth. Father Michael shared stories of individuals who had experienced similar crises and found renewed meaning and purpose through their struggles.

One of the most impactful insights Father Michael provided was the idea that faith could be rekindled through acts of service and compassion. He encouraged Emily to engage in community service and volunteer work as a way to connect with others and rediscover the value of spiritual principles in action. He emphasized that faith was not merely a set of beliefs but a lived experience that could be enriched through meaningful connections with others.

The Path to Renewal

Inspired by Father Michael's guidance, Emily began to approach her faith with a renewed perspective. She started by participating in community service projects, including volunteering at a local shelter and organizing fundraising events for charitable causes. Through these activities, she discovered a sense of fulfillment and purpose that she had been missing.

Emily also re-engaged with her religious community, albeit with a new outlook. She attended services and participated in study groups, not as a means of rigid adherence but as an opportunity for exploration and dialogue. She approached her spiritual practices with an open mind, seeking to integrate the lessons and values she had learned from her diverse experiences.

As she immersed herself in acts of service and spiritual practice, Emily began to experience a shift in her perspective. She found that her faith was not a fixed doctrine but a living, evolving journey. Her understanding of spirituality became more inclusive and compassionate, incorporating elements from her previous experiences and new insights.

Emily also developed a deeper appreciation for the role of faith in providing hope and comfort during challenging times. She recognized that her struggles and doubts were part of a broader human experience and that faith could offer a source of strength and resilience. Her renewed faith was not about returning to a previous state of belief but about embracing a more nuanced and profound understanding of spirituality.

The Impact on Personal Growth

The journey from doubt to enlightenment had a profound impact on Emily's personal growth. She learned valuable lessons about resilience, self-discovery, and the transformative power of faith. Her experience illustrated the importance of embracing uncertainty and vulnerability as part of the spiritual journey.

One of the key lessons Emily learned was the value of patience and perseverance. Her path to renewal was not immediate or straightforward. It required time, effort, and openness to new experiences. Emily's willingness to explore different perspectives and engage in self-reflection allowed her to overcome her doubts and develop a more profound understanding of her faith. Emily also discovered the importance of community and support in the spiritual journey. Her interactions with Father Michael and her involvement in community service helped her build meaningful connections with others and reinforced the idea that faith is enriched through shared experiences and acts of compassion.

Moreover, Emily's renewed faith empowered her to approach challenges with a sense of purpose and hope. She developed a greater sense of clarity about her values and goals, which guided her decisions and actions. Her experience highlighted the potential for faith to inspire positive change and contribute to personal and communal well-being.

Broader Implications

Emily's story offers valuable insights into the nature of faith and the process of overcoming doubts and struggles. It illustrates that faith is not a static or monolithic concept but a dynamic and evolving journey. Her experience underscores the importance of approaching spiritual crises with openness, humility, and a willingness to explore new perspectives.

The lessons from Emily's journey are relevant not only to individuals facing crises of faith but also to those navigating other personal and spiritual challenges. The principles of resilience, community support, and self-discovery can be applied to various aspects of life, including relationships, career development, and personal growth.

Emily's story also highlights the importance of seeking guidance and support during times of doubt. Her encounters with Father Michael and her involvement in community service provided her with valuable insights and opportunities for renewal. This emphasizes the role of mentors, spiritual leaders, and supportive communities in helping individuals navigate their spiritual journeys.

Conclusion

"The Lost Faith" is a compelling story of a young woman's journey from doubt and disillusionment to spiritual renewal and enlightenment. Emily's experience demonstrates the transformative power of faith and the potential for personal growth through struggles and challenges. Her story offers valuable lessons about the nature of faith, the importance of community and support, and the process of overcoming doubts.

Through her journey, Emily discovered that faith is not a fixed or rigid concept but a dynamic and evolving journey. Her renewed faith was characterized by a deeper understanding of spirituality, a greater appreciation for acts of service and compassion, and a more inclusive and compassionate perspective. Emily's story serves as a reminder of the resilience of the human spirit and the potential for faith to inspire positive change and personal growth.

CHAPTER 10

THE ILLNESS: A TALE OF FAITH, HEALING, AND REDEMPTION

In a serene village surrounded by rolling hills and verdant fields, the peaceful life of its residents was disrupted by a profound crisis. The tale centers around Lydia, a young woman whose life took an unexpected turn due to a debilitating illness. This narrative is more than just a story of physical suffering; it is a journey through faith, hope, and redemption, exploring how Lydia's illness led to profound spiritual and personal transformation.

Lydia's Life Before the Illness

Before the onset of her illness, Lydia lived a life that many would consider ideal. She was a dedicated teacher at the local school, known for her kindness and commitment to her students. Her days were filled with teaching, community involvement, and a close-knit circle of friends and family. Lydia's faith was an integral part of her life; she attended church regularly, participated in Bible study groups, and was actively involved in charity work.

Lydia's faith was strong and unwavering. She believed in the power of prayer, the healing touch of divine grace, and the comfort that her religious community provided. Her life was a testament to the harmony between her personal beliefs and her daily actions. She found joy in serving others and believed that her faith guided her in every aspect of her life.

The Onset of Illness

The tranquility of Lydia's life was shattered when she began experiencing persistent and unexplained symptoms. Initially, it started with fatigue and frequent headaches, which she attributed to the demands of her busy schedule. However, as the symptoms worsened, Lydia sought medical advice. Tests revealed that she was suffering from a rare and severe illness that required immediate and intensive treatment.

The diagnosis was a devastating blow. Lydia's illness was not only physically debilitating but also emotionally challenging. The treatment regimen was harsh and demanding, involving frequent hospital visits, complex medications, and significant lifestyle adjustments. Lydia's once vibrant and active life became constrained by her condition. The illness took a toll on her ability to teach, participate in community activities, and maintain her previous level of engagement with her faith.

The Struggle with Faith

As Lydia grappled with her illness, her faith was put to the test. The harsh realities of her condition led her to question the very beliefs that had once been her source of strength. She struggled with feelings of abandonment and doubt. The prayers that had once brought her comfort now seemed unanswered, and the divine grace she had always relied upon felt distant.

During this period of intense struggle, Lydia experienced a range of emotions—fear, anger, and frustration. She wondered why she had been chosen to endure such suffering and why her prayers seemed to go unheard. The sense of isolation and helplessness intensified as she faced the harsh realities of her illness. Her previously unshakable faith was now marred by uncertainty and despair.

Lydia's spiritual community rallied around her, offering prayers, support, and encouragement. Yet, despite their best efforts, Lydia felt disconnected from the very faith that had once been her anchor. The disconnect was not just with her spiritual beliefs but also with the community that had always been a source of solace and support.

The Turning Point

The turning point in Lydia's journey came when she decided to take a step back and re-evaluate her approach to faith and healing. Recognizing the need for a new perspective, she began to explore different ways to reconnect with her spirituality. This period of introspection and exploration marked a significant shift in her understanding of faith and healing.

Lydia started by reading spiritual texts and engaging in reflective practices that were different from her usual routine. She read about individuals from various religious traditions who had faced profound suffering and found renewed meaning through their experiences. She also began keeping a journal, documenting her thoughts, feelings, and reflections on her spiritual journey.

During this period, Lydia encountered a passage from the Bible that resonated deeply with her. It was from the Book of Job, a story of profound suffering and eventual restoration. The passage spoke of enduring faith amidst trials and the eventual vindication of righteousness. Lydia found solace in Job's story, seeing parallels between his experience and her own.

This newfound perspective encouraged Lydia to adopt a more contemplative and open approach to her faith. She began to view her illness not as a punishment or abandonment but as a part of a larger journey of spiritual growth and understanding. Her focus shifted from seeking immediate answers to embracing the process of spiritual transformation.

The Role of Community and Support

Throughout her illness, Lydia's community played a crucial role in her healing journey. While she initially felt disconnected from her faith community, their unwavering support became an essential element of her recovery process. Their presence, prayers, and acts of kindness helped her regain a sense of belonging and hope.

One of the most significant sources of support came from a group of friends who organized regular visits, providing emotional comfort and practical assistance. They helped Lydia with daily tasks, offered companionship, and shared their own experiences of faith and healing. This support network became a source of strength, reminding Lydia of the importance of human connection in times of adversity.

Additionally, Lydia's interactions with her pastor and spiritual advisor provided her with valuable insights and guidance. Her pastor encouraged her to explore different dimensions of faith and spirituality, emphasizing that healing was not just a physical process but also a spiritual one. Through conversations and prayers, Lydia was able to find new meaning in her suffering and develop a deeper understanding of her faith.

The Journey of Healing and Redemption

As Lydia continued her journey of faith and healing, she experienced gradual improvements in her physical condition. The medical treatments began to show positive results, and she found renewed energy and strength. However, the healing process was not solely physical; it was deeply intertwined with her spiritual and emotional growth.

Lydia's journey towards redemption was characterized by several key elements:

1. Embracing Imperfection: Lydia learned to accept her vulnerability and imperfection. She realized that her faith did not require her to be flawless or invulnerable but to be open to growth and transformation. This acceptance allowed her to find peace in the midst of her struggles and to embrace her journey with grace.

2. Finding Meaning in Suffering: Through her reflections and spiritual exploration, Lydia began to find meaning in her suffering. She understood that her illness was an opportunity for personal and spiritual growth. This shift in perspective helped her approach her recovery with a sense of purpose and acceptance.

3. Reconnecting with Faith: Lydia's renewed faith was characterized by a deeper and more nuanced understanding of spirituality. She embraced the idea that faith could be a source of strength even in the face of unanswered prayers and challenges. Her relationship with her faith evolved from one of expectation to one of trust and surrender.

4. Strengthening Community Bonds: The support and companionship of her community played a vital role in Lydia's healing journey. She recognized the value of shared experiences and mutual support in the process of recovery. Her renewed appreciation for community strengthened her connections with others and reinforced her sense of belonging.

5. Living with Gratitude: Lydia developed a profound sense of gratitude for the lessons learned through her illness. She appreciated the beauty of life's simple moments and the strength that emerged from her struggles. This gratitude became a central aspect of her renewed faith and outlook on life.

The Legacy of Lydia's Journey

Lydia's journey of faith, healing, and redemption had a lasting impact on her life and the lives of those around her. Her story became a source of inspiration for others facing similar struggles, demonstrating the power of faith and resilience in overcoming adversity.

Lydia's experience also led her to become an advocate for others dealing with illness and suffering. She began sharing her story with local support groups and engaging in community outreach to offer hope and encouragement. Her insights and experiences provided valuable guidance to those navigating their own spiritual and emotional challenges.

In addition, Lydia's renewed faith and perspective influenced her teaching and community involvement. She integrated her experiences into her work, emphasizing the importance of compassion, resilience, and the transformative power of faith. Her approach to teaching and community service became more empathetic and holistic, reflecting the lessons learned through her own journey.

Broader Implications

The story of Lydia's illness and recovery offers broader insights into the nature of faith, healing, and personal growth. It highlights several key themes and principles that are relevant to various aspects of life:

1. The Role of Faith in Healing: Lydia's journey underscores the role of faith in the healing process. Faith can provide comfort, purpose, and strength during times of adversity. It can also offer a framework for understanding and accepting suffering as part of a broader spiritual journey.
2. The Importance of Community Support: The support of a compassionate and engaged community is crucial for individuals facing illness and challenges. Community bonds can provide emotional comfort, practical assistance, and a sense of belonging.

3. The Value of Personal Growth: Suffering and adversity can lead to significant personal and spiritual growth. Embracing challenges with an open and reflective mindset can lead to profound insights and a deeper understanding of oneself and one's beliefs.
4. The Significance of Gratitude: Developing a sense of gratitude for life's lessons and experiences can enhance personal well-being and spiritual fulfillment. Gratitude helps individuals find meaning and appreciation in the midst of difficulties.
5. The Power of Resilience: Lydia's story illustrates the power of resilience in overcoming adversity. Resilience involves the ability to adapt, grow, and find strength in the face of challenges. It is a key component of the healing process and personal transformation.

Conclusion

"The Illness" is a poignant and inspiring tale of faith, healing, and redemption. Lydia's journey from a vibrant life to a period of profound struggle and eventual renewal illustrates the transformative power of faith and resilience. Her story offers valuable lessons about the nature of suffering, the importance of community support, and the potential for personal and spiritual growth.

Through her experiences, Lydia discovered a deeper and more nuanced understanding of her faith, finding meaning and purpose in her suffering. Her journey serves as a powerful reminder of the strength and grace that can emerge from the challenges we face and the profound impact of faith and community in the healing process.

CHAPTER 11

THE FINANCIAL STRAIN: A STORY OF PERSEVERANCE AND REDEMPTION

Financial strain is a formidable challenge that affects countless individuals and families across the globe. It is a situation that can test one's resilience, strain relationships, and impact overall well-being. This story delves into the life of Michael and Emily, a couple whose journey through severe financial hardship became a testament to perseverance, faith, and eventual redemption.

Michael and Emily's Life Before Financial Strain

Michael and Emily were a young couple living in a vibrant city. Both were hardworking professionals—Michael worked as a software engineer, while Emily was a marketing manager. Their lives were characterized by a sense of stability and ambition. They enjoyed the comforts of a well-furnished apartment, had a modest savings account, and looked forward to a promising future.

Their financial stability allowed them to enjoy a comfortable lifestyle. They traveled occasionally, dined out with friends, and participated in various social activities. They were also diligent savers, setting aside funds for future goals such as buying a home and starting a family. Their financial outlook seemed secure, and they felt confident in their ability to manage their finances effectively.

The Onset of Financial Hardship

The first signs of financial trouble emerged gradually. Michael's company underwent restructuring, leading to job losses and a freeze on salary increases. He was among those affected, and his position was eliminated. This sudden loss of income was the beginning of a challenging period for the couple. Although Michael received a severance package, it was not sufficient to cover their living expenses for an extended period.

Emily's job, though stable, did not provide enough additional income to compensate for Michael's lost salary. The couple's initial response was to cut back on non-essential expenses. They reduced dining out, postponed travel plans, and scrutinized their monthly budget. Despite their efforts, the financial strain continued to escalate.

As Michael searched for new employment, he faced a highly competitive job market. The delay in securing a new position further exacerbated their financial difficulties. They began to deplete their savings, which had once seemed like a safety net. The stress of their diminishing financial resources began to affect their relationship and overall well-being.

The Emotional and Psychological Impact

The financial strain took a significant toll on Michael and Emily's emotional and psychological well-being. The constant worry about making ends meet led to sleepless nights and increased anxiety. They found themselves arguing more frequently, with financial stress becoming a focal point of their disagreements. The pressure of managing bills, mortgages, and other financial obligations created an atmosphere of tension and uncertainty.

Emily, in particular, struggled with feelings of guilt and frustration. She felt responsible for maintaining financial stability and worried about the future. The burden of their financial problems affected her self-esteem and confidence. Michael, on the other hand, grappled with feelings of inadequacy and failure. The job search was disheartening, and the lack of progress made him feel disheartened and demoralized.

The emotional strain also impacted their social life. They withdrew from friends and family, feeling embarrassed and ashamed of their situation. The isolation added to their sense of helplessness and deepened their struggles.

Seeking Solutions

Realizing that their financial situation was unsustainable, Michael and Emily sought various solutions to alleviate their strain. They consulted with a financial advisor who helped them create a more manageable budget and explore options for restructuring their debt. The advisor recommended prioritizing essential expenses, renegotiating loan terms, and exploring potential sources of additional income.

In addition to professional financial advice, the couple considered alternative ways to improve their financial situation. Michael took on freelance work and temporary projects to generate supplementary income. Emily explored opportunities for career advancement and additional part-time work. They also sought assistance from community resources, including local charities and support organizations that offered financial counseling and emergency aid.

The process of seeking solutions was both challenging and empowering. Michael and Emily realized that they needed to confront their financial issues head-on and take proactive steps to address them. Their efforts were not without setbacks, but they remained determined to overcome their difficulties.

Rebuilding and Recovery

The journey to financial recovery was gradual and required persistence and patience. Michael eventually secured a new full-time job, which provided a stable income and an opportunity to rebuild their financial foundation. Emily continued to work diligently in her role and took on additional projects to bolster their financial stability.

As they began to see improvements in their financial situation, Michael and Emily focused on rebuilding their savings and stabilizing their budget. They set new financial goals, including creating an emergency fund and planning for future expenses. Their experience taught them valuable lessons about financial management, resilience, and the importance of maintaining a positive outlook.

The couple also worked on repairing and strengthening their relationship. They sought couples counseling to address the emotional strain caused by their financial difficulties. Through therapy, they learned effective communication strategies, developed coping mechanisms for stress, and reconnected on an emotional level.

Their journey of rebuilding was marked by a renewed sense of purpose and hope. Michael and Emily's experience with financial strain became a catalyst for personal growth and transformation. They developed a deeper understanding of their own strengths and limitations and gained a greater appreciation for the support of their community and each other.

Lessons Learned

Michael and Emily's experience with financial strain imparted several important lessons:

1. Financial Planning and Preparedness: One of the key lessons learned was the importance of proactive financial planning and preparedness. Having a well-structured budget, savings plan, and contingency fund can provide a safety net during times of economic uncertainty.

2. Resilience and Adaptability: The couple's journey highlighted the importance of resilience and adaptability in the face of financial challenges. Their ability to seek solutions, make necessary adjustments, and remain hopeful despite setbacks played a crucial role in their recovery.

3. Communication and Support: Effective communication and support were essential in navigating the emotional and psychological impact of financial strain. Michael and Emily's efforts to seek counseling and strengthen their relationship underscored the significance of maintaining open dialogue and mutual support.

4. Community Resources: The availability of community resources and support organizations proved invaluable in their journey. Seeking assistance from local charities and financial counseling services provided them with practical solutions and emotional support.

5. Personal Growth: The experience of financial strain led to significant personal and relational growth. Michael and Emily emerged from their challenges with a deeper understanding of themselves and each other, as well as a renewed sense of purpose and gratitude.

The Broader Implications

The story of Michael and Emily's financial strain serves as a microcosm of broader societal issues related to economic hardship. It reflects the challenges faced by many individuals and families dealing with financial difficulties and the profound impact that such challenges can have on various aspects of life.

1. Economic Vulnerability: The story illustrates the vulnerability that individuals and families face in times of economic instability. Job loss, unexpected expenses, and financial setbacks can have far-reaching consequences, affecting not only financial stability but also emotional well-being and relationships.

2. Support Systems: The importance of support systems, including community resources, professional guidance, and social networks, is evident in the couple's journey. Access to support can significantly impact an individual's ability to navigate financial challenges and achieve recovery.

3. Mental Health and Well-Being: Financial strain often intersects with mental health and overall well-being. The emotional and psychological impact of financial difficulties underscores the need for addressing mental health concerns alongside financial challenges.

4. Education and Awareness: The story highlights the need for education and awareness regarding financial management and planning. Empowering individuals with knowledge and skills to manage their finances effectively can help mitigate the impact of financial strain.

Conclusion

"The Financial Strain" is a compelling narrative of perseverance, resilience, and redemption. Michael and Emily's journey through financial hardship and their eventual recovery exemplify the strength of the human spirit and the importance of faith, support, and personal growth in overcoming adversity.

Their story serves as a powerful reminder of the challenges faced by many individuals dealing with financial difficulties and the broader implications of such challenges. It underscores the need for proactive financial planning, effective communication, and community support in navigating economic hardships.

Ultimately, Michael and Emily's experience is a testament to the possibility of transformation and renewal in the face of financial strain. Their journey highlights the capacity for growth, healing, and hope, offering valuable lessons for others facing similar challenges.

CHAPTER 12

THE DIFFICULT TASK: A JOURNEY OF PERSEVERANCE AND REDEMPTION

The story of the difficult task is not just a narrative about overcoming challenges but a profound exploration of perseverance, faith, and personal growth. It is a journey that reflects the struggles many face when confronted with seemingly insurmountable obstacles and the strength required to navigate these trials. This story delves deeply into the experiences of individuals who undertake arduous tasks and emerge transformed, illustrating the power of determination and the impact of support systems.

The Prelude to Challenge

Our story begins with Elena, a dedicated single mother living in a small town. Elena worked as a nurse, balancing the demands of her job with the responsibilities of raising her young daughter, Sophie. Life for Elena was characterized by a relentless pursuit of stability and security for her family. Despite her tireless efforts, she found herself constantly juggling work, childcare, and household duties.

Elena's life took a dramatic turn when she was diagnosed with a serious health condition that required surgery. The diagnosis was a heavy blow, not only because of the health implications but also due to the financial strain it imposed. The medical bills, combined with her inability to work during her recovery, placed Elena in an increasingly precarious situation.

As she faced this new reality, Elena felt overwhelmed by the enormity of the task ahead. The combination of managing her health, supporting her daughter, and handling the financial burden seemed daunting. However, Elena's deep love for Sophie and her determination to overcome the challenge fueled her resolve.

The Nature of the Task

The task before Elena was multifaceted and complex. It involved not only managing her health and financial situation but also maintaining her role as a mother. The intricacies of this task included:

1. Medical Recovery: Elena needed to undergo surgery, followed by a period of recovery that required rest and medical care. The uncertainty of her recovery and the potential for complications added to her anxiety.

2. Financial Management: With mounting medical bills and the inability to work, Elena had to navigate a complex financial landscape. This included managing existing debts, seeking financial assistance, and budgeting for essential expenses.

3. Parenting: As a single mother, Elena's responsibility to care for Sophie was a constant priority. Balancing her own recovery with meeting Sophie's needs required meticulous planning and support.

4. Emotional Resilience: The emotional toll of dealing with a serious health condition, financial stress, and parenting responsibilities demanded significant emotional resilience. Elena needed to stay positive and focused despite the numerous challenges she faced.

The Struggle and the Search for Solutions

Elena's journey through the difficult task was marked by numerous struggles and moments of doubt. The initial phase was characterized by intense physical pain, emotional distress, and financial anxiety. Despite her efforts to remain optimistic, the cumulative weight of these challenges began to take a toll.

In seeking solutions, Elena reached out to various resources and support systems:

1. Medical Support: Elena worked closely with her healthcare providers to ensure she received the best possible care. They provided guidance on managing her condition, addressing complications, and navigating the recovery process.

2. Financial Assistance: Elena sought assistance from local charities and support organizations that offered financial aid to individuals facing medical crises. She also explored options for government assistance and negotiated payment plans with medical providers.

3. Community Support: Recognizing the importance of community support, Elena reached out to friends, family, and local support groups. Their encouragement, practical help, and emotional support played a crucial role in alleviating her burden.

4. Self-Care and Resilience: Elena focused on self-care strategies to maintain her emotional and mental well-being. She practiced mindfulness, sought counseling, and engaged in activities that helped her manage stress and stay resilient.

The Role of Faith and Community

Throughout her journey, Elena's faith and the support of her community were instrumental in helping her navigate the difficult task. Her faith provided her with a sense of hope and purpose, while the support of those around her offered practical and emotional assistance.

1. Faith: Elena's faith was a source of comfort and strength. It provided her with a sense of purpose and hope during challenging times. Her belief in a higher power and the support of her religious community offered her solace and encouragement.

2. Community: The support from friends, family, and local organizations was vital. They helped with practical tasks such as meal preparation, childcare, and household chores. Their emotional support, including regular check-ins and encouragement, helped Elena stay positive and focused.

3. Shared Experiences: Connecting with others who had faced similar challenges offered Elena valuable insights and encouragement. Hearing stories of perseverance and recovery inspired her and provided practical advice for managing her situation.

The Transformation and Redemption

As Elena navigated the difficult task, she experienced a profound transformation. The journey was marked by moments of hardship and struggle, but it also led to significant personal growth and redemption.

1. Personal Growth: Elena's experience taught her the importance of resilience, adaptability, and self-compassion. She developed a deeper understanding of her own strengths and limitations and learned to embrace vulnerability and seek support.

2. Strengthening Relationships: The challenges she faced strengthened her relationships with friends, family, and her daughter. The support she received deepened her connections with others and highlighted the importance of community and mutual support.

3. Renewed Perspective: Elena emerged from her experience with a renewed perspective on life. She developed a greater appreciation for the small joys and the importance of focusing on what truly matters. Her journey of overcoming adversity instilled in her a sense of gratitude and purpose.

4. Empowerment: Through her struggles, Elena gained a sense of empowerment. She learned that even in the face of daunting challenges,

she had the strength and resilience to overcome adversity. This newfound empowerment gave her the confidence to face future challenges with optimism and determination.

Lessons and Broader Implications

Elena's story provides valuable lessons and insights that extend beyond her personal experience. It highlights the broader implications of facing difficult tasks and the importance of perseverance, faith, and support systems.

1. Resilience in Adversity: The story underscores the importance of resilience when facing adversity. It demonstrates that challenges, while daunting, can be overcome with determination, adaptability, and a positive mindset.

2. The Power of Support Systems: The role of community and support systems is a central theme in Elena's journey. It emphasizes the importance of seeking help and building strong support networks during difficult times.

3. The Impact of Faith: Elena's faith played a significant role in her ability to persevere. The story highlights the power of faith in providing hope, purpose, and emotional strength during challenging times.

4. Personal Growth Through Challenges: The narrative illustrates how challenges can lead to personal growth and transformation. It emphasizes that overcoming adversity can result in increased self-awareness, strength, and a renewed perspective on life.

5. Empowerment Through Struggle: Elena's journey demonstrates how facing and overcoming difficulties can lead to empowerment and confidence. It highlights the importance of embracing challenges as opportunities for growth and self-discovery.

Conclusion

The story of Elena's difficult task is a compelling narrative of perseverance, faith, and personal growth. Her journey through health challenges, financial strain, and parenting responsibilities illustrates the strength required to navigate adversity and the profound impact of support systems and faith.

Elena's experience serves as a powerful reminder of the resilience of the human spirit and the transformative power of overcoming challenges. Her story highlights the importance of seeking support, maintaining faith, and embracing personal growth through difficult times. Ultimately, it offers valuable lessons for others facing similar challenges, demonstrating that even the most daunting tasks can be overcome with determination, support, and a positive outlook.

CHAPTER 13

THE BROKEN FRIENDSHIP: A TALE OF LOSS, GROWTH, AND RECONCILIATION

Friendships are among the most cherished relationships in our lives, providing us with companionship, support, and joy. However, even the closest of friendships can face trials and fractures. "The Broken Friendship" is a story that explores the complexities of such a relationship, revealing the deep emotional impacts of estrangement and the profound journey of healing and reconciliation. This narrative reflects on how the fractures in a friendship can lead to personal growth and a renewed understanding of the importance of forgiveness and empathy.

The Foundation of Friendship

The story centers on Rachel and Laura, two childhood friends who shared a bond that seemed unbreakable. Their friendship began in early school years, blossoming through shared experiences, laughter, and mutual support. Rachel and Laura were inseparable; they celebrated each other's successes, comforted one another through hardships, and created a myriad of cherished memories.

Their friendship was built on a foundation of trust and understanding. They confided in each other, supported each other's dreams, and navigated the challenges of adolescence and early adulthood together. Their connection was deep and unwavering, seemingly impervious to the typical strains of life.

The Catalyst for Conflict

The harmony of Rachel and Laura's friendship began to fray as they entered adulthood. The pressures of life, including career ambitions, romantic relationships, and differing life choices, began to create a subtle distance between them. The differences in their priorities and perspectives started to emerge, leading to occasional misunderstandings and disagreements.

The real catalyst for the conflict, however, was a particular event that exposed the vulnerabilities in their relationship. Rachel and Laura had planned a significant celebration for Laura's milestone birthday. Rachel, who was deeply involved in her career and personal commitments, struggled to find time to fully contribute to the planning. Laura, feeling overwhelmed by the preparations and perceiving Rachel's lack of involvement as a sign of disinterest, felt deeply hurt and betrayed.

This event marked the beginning of a series of misunderstandings and unmet expectations. Laura's feelings of resentment grew, and Rachel's attempts to explain her situation were met with defensiveness. The lack of communication and the accumulation of unresolved issues led to a dramatic fallout. The friendship, once robust and resilient, began to unravel.

The Fallout and Estrangement

The aftermath of their fallout was marked by a painful period of estrangement. Both Rachel and Laura felt deeply hurt and confused by the breakdown of their once-cherished relationship. The friendship that had been a constant source of support and joy had suddenly become a source of emotional turmoil and regret. During this period of estrangement, Rachel and Laura each grappled with their feelings of loss and betrayal. Rachel felt remorseful and confused about how things had deteriorated so quickly. She missed Laura's presence in her life and struggled with guilt over her perceived failings. Laura, on the other hand, felt a mix of anger and sadness. She was hurt by what she perceived as Rachel's lack of commitment and felt that the friendship had been one-sided.

The estrangement led to a significant emotional burden for both. Rachel and Laura were both left with unresolved feelings and a longing for the connection they once shared. The absence of their friendship left a void in their lives, affecting their emotional well-being and personal happiness.

The Path to Reconciliation

As time passed, Rachel and Laura began to reflect on their friendship and the events that led to its breakdown. Both recognized that their estrangement had created a deep sense of loss and regret. They realized that the issues between them were not insurmountable and that the friendship they once valued was worth the effort to repair.

The path to reconciliation began with introspection and self-awareness. Rachel and Laura each took the time to understand their own roles in the conflict and the underlying emotions that had driven their reactions. They both acknowledged their mistakes and recognized the need for open and honest communication.

1. Reaching Out: The first step towards reconciliation involved reaching out. Rachel took the initiative to contact Laura, expressing her sincere desire to address their issues and rebuild their friendship. This gesture was met with mixed emotions, but it marked the beginning of a crucial dialogue.

2. Open Communication: Rachel and Laura engaged in open and honest conversations about their feelings, expectations, and grievances. They discussed the misunderstandings and hurtful incidents that had led to their estrangement. This process of communication allowed them to express their emotions and gain a deeper understanding of each other's perspectives.

3. Apologies and Forgiveness: Both Rachel and Laura offered apologies for their respective roles in the conflict. Rachel apologized for her perceived lack of involvement and the hurt it caused Laura. Laura apologized for her assumptions and the way she reacted to the situation. The process of apologizing and seeking forgiveness was a significant step towards healing and rebuilding trust.

4. Rebuilding Trust: Rebuilding trust required time and consistent effort. Rachel and Laura made a conscious effort to reconnect and reestablish their bond. They engaged in activities that they had once enjoyed together and worked on creating new positive experiences. Their efforts to rebuild trust were marked by patience and mutual respect.

5. Learning and Growth: The reconciliation process also involved learning from their experiences. Rachel and Laura reflected on the lessons they had learned about themselves and their friendship. They recognized the importance of communication, empathy, and managing expectations in maintaining a healthy relationship.

The Impact of Reconciliation

The process of reconciliation had a profound impact on both Rachel and Laura. It transformed their understanding of friendship and their approach to handling conflicts and challenges. The journey of mending their relationship led to several key outcomes:

1. Strengthened Bond: Rachel and Laura's reconciliation resulted in a strengthened bond. Their renewed friendship was built on a deeper understanding and appreciation of each other. They emerged from their difficulties with a more resilient and enduring connection.

2. Personal Growth: The experience of navigating conflict and reconciliation led to significant personal growth for both Rachel and Laura. They developed greater emotional maturity, improved

communication skills, and a deeper understanding of their own needs and boundaries.

3. Renewed Appreciation: The process of reconciliation deepened their appreciation for each other. They came to value their friendship more profoundly and recognized the importance of nurturing and maintaining their relationship.

4. Healing and Forgiveness: The act of forgiving and seeking forgiveness provided a sense of emotional relief and closure. It allowed Rachel and Laura to let go of past grievances and move forward with a renewed sense of hope and optimism.

Broader Lessons and Implications

The story of Rachel and Laura's broken friendship and reconciliation offers several broader lessons and implications:

1. The Importance of Communication: Effective communication is crucial in maintaining healthy relationships. Open and honest dialogue can help address misunderstandings and prevent conflicts from escalating.

2. The Role of Forgiveness: Forgiveness is a powerful tool in healing and rebuilding relationships. It involves acknowledging mistakes, offering sincere apologies, and letting go of resentment. Forgiveness can pave the way for emotional healing and renewal.

3. The Impact of Personal Growth: Navigating conflicts and challenges can lead to personal growth and self-awareness. The process of addressing issues and seeking reconciliation can help individuals develop greater emotional resilience and maturity.

4. The Value of Relationships: Friendships and relationships are valuable and worth investing in. The story underscores the importance of nurturing connections and the rewards of working through difficulties to maintain meaningful relationships.

5. The Power of Empathy: Empathy plays a critical role in understanding and resolving conflicts. By putting themselves in each other's shoes, Rachel and Laura were able to gain insight into each other's perspectives and work towards a resolution.

Conclusion

"The Broken Friendship" is a poignant tale of loss, growth, and reconciliation. It highlights the complexities of navigating conflicts in close relationships and the transformative power of forgiveness and communication. Rachel and Laura's journey from estrangement to reconciliation serves as a testament to the strength of enduring friendships and the importance of addressing challenges with empathy and understanding.

Their story offers valuable lessons about the nature of relationships, the role of personal growth in overcoming adversity, and the importance of nurturing connections. It reminds us that even when friendships face significant trials, the effort to repair and rebuild can lead to profound growth and a renewed appreciation for the bonds we cherish.

I want morebooks!

Buy your books fast and straightforward online - at one of world's fastest growing online book stores! Environmentally sound due to Print-on-Demand technologies.

Buy your books online at
www.morebooks.shop

Kaufen Sie Ihre Bücher schnell und unkompliziert online – auf einer der am schnellsten wachsenden Buchhandelsplattformen weltweit! Dank Print-On-Demand umwelt- und ressourcenschonend produziert.

Bücher schneller online kaufen
www.morebooks.shop

Printed by Books on Demand GmbH, Norderstedt / Germany